Center for Basque Studies
Current Research Series, No. 1

Equality, Equity, and Diversity: Educational Solutions in the Basque Country

Edited by
Alfonso Unceta and Concepción Medrano

Current Research Series No. 1

Translated by Ines Swaney

Center for Basque Studies
University of Nevada, Reno

Published in conjunction with the University of the Basque Country
UPV/EHU

Current Research
Selections of the ongoing work done by the faculty of the University of the Basque Country (UPV/EHU)

Editorial Committee
Amaia Maseda (Chair, UPV/EHU), Arantza Azpiroz (UPV/EHU), Javier Echeverría (Ikerbasque), Jon Landeta (UPV/EHU), Sandra Ott (UNR), Joseba Zulaika (UNR), Santos Zunzunegui (UPV/EHU)

Current Research Series, No. 1

Center for Basque Studies
University of Nevada, Reno
Reno, Nevada 89557
http://basque.unr.edu

Cover and series design © 2010 by Jose Luis Agote.
Cover design based on engravings by Eduardo Chillida and Jorge Oteiza.

Library of Congress Cataloging-in-Publication Data

Equality, equity, and diversity : educational solutions in the Basque Country / edited by Alfonso Unceta and Concepción Medrano.
    p. cm.
"Published in conjunction with the University of the Basque Country."
Includes bibliographical references and index.
Summary: "Collection of articles on education in the Basque Country"-- Provided by publisher.
ISBN 978-1-935709-00-8 (pbk.)
1. Education--Spain--País Vasco. 2. Educational equalization--Spain-- País Vasco. I. Unceta, Alfonso. II. Medrano, Concepción. III. Title.

LA919.P34E68 2010
370.946'6--dc22

2010036941

Contents

Introduction

Alfonso Unceta and Concepción Medrano

Education, considered an essential human right, provides the possibility of a complete development of individuals, and also for making progress in the structuring of more impartial societies. Therefore, generalized access to schooling is possibly one of the greatest achievements of European countries during the past twentieth century. However, educational systems are neither exclusive agents in the formation of citizens, nor is their existence sufficient to alleviate social, economic and cultural imbalances present in our current intercultural societies.

These imbalances are typical in Western society, therefore European countries as a whole are facing similar problems within a context of an accelerated change in the values, beliefs and attitudes of their citizenry. The educational and developmental task required by our social reality is not exclusively the responsibility of what is known as *formal education*, but must be shared with other agents including to a considerable extent families and the media.

In addition, education has increasingly become a strategic factor for mitigating social imbalance situations in our societies, as well as for promoting the necessary civic and ethical upbringing of our citizens. Hence, educational projects that attribute an essential value to equality and fairness stress the importance of diversity and promoting social and human values, starting with respect for basic human rights. And—as has already been stated—this huge educational and developmental task must be approached from the standpoint of cooperation between several agents, in addition to responding to the needs and interest of quite diverse groups.

The Basque Country, fully embedded within the European context, faces similar educational challenges to these. From the political-administrative standpoint, what is currently known as the Basque Country consists of an autonomous community[1] with a population of slightly more than 2.1 million, geographically made up of three provinces: Bizkaia (Vizcaya, population 1,150,000), Gipuzkoa (Guipúzcoa, 690,000), and Araba (Álava, 310,000). An intricate network has been developed within these three provinces consisting of more than 250 local entities (municipalities). Beyond the municipal and provincial government institutions, since 1980 the Basque government has had full powers to develop educational policies, in applying the statute of autonomy of the Comunidad Autónoma del País Vasco/ Euskal Autonomia Erkidegoa (CAPV/EAE, Autonomous Community of the Basque Country), passed by the Spanish parliament in 1979.

This authority allows the Basque Country to design and execute educational policies, a privileged course of action on the part of governments and a mirror reflecting their priorities and those of the societies they represent. In the case of the CAPV/EAE, it is a society that enjoys a quite extended and consolidated general status of wellbeing, which nevertheless coexists with certain social, cultural and economic inequities affecting varied social groups. This is quite typical in those advanced societies where development and scarcity coexist in an increasingly complex arena. And the administration of this complexity finds within education a privileged setting whereby to promote equality and fairness.

Hence the educational initiatives aimed at achieving greater equality and fairness in our society are extremely relevant and are reflected in various social settings which, moreover, interact among themselves: both within the core of the educational system, because the extraordinary diversity and heterogeneity of the student body is an unending source of problems and tensions; and in society in general, because—as has already been pointed out—the situations of inequality between individuals and groups are also part of the social landscape in the Basque Country.

In this latter sense, the text we present here brings together general observations as well as educational research and answers specifically aimed at achieving a more satisfactory situation of equality and fairness.

---

1. Upon approval of the 1978 Spanish Constitution, the Spanish state became known as a state of the autonomies, with seventeen autonomous communities having ample administrative authority as the result of a transfer of powers from the central state (some as important as educational and sanitation powers, among others).

In some cases, they are anchored, posed or developed within exclusively educational spheres; in other cases, within broader social settings. Altogether, various instructors and researchers from the Universidad del País Vasco/Euskal Herriko Unibertsitatea (UPV/EHU, University of the Basque Country) provide here an outlook combining theoretical and analytical dimensions and direct involvement in the growth of programs developed, in most cases, during the last decade (since 2000). Prior to their final acceptance and inclusion in this volume, all papers have undergone two independent outside evaluations performed by experts in the field. Taken as a whole, the text is a synthesis of experiences, records and data, that when analyzed in their entirety provides us with an all-encompassing view on the topic; in other words, a complementary view from both a socio-educational and a school context.

The educational context frames the first part of the volume, made up of five chapters. In recent years, schools have obviously become an arena for a wide range of activities linked to the goals of equality and fairness. These activities are similar in their general goals, but different in terms of the specific thematic they address. In this regard, themes are varied although they remain interrelated. For example, the assignment and use of resources for promoting educational fairness; the analysis of the level of fairness in educational processes and results; the development of broad curricular themes; or the answers to diversity in the classrooms by means of curricular adaptations or curricular diversification programs, are just some expressions wherein educational responses might be applied.

Given this situation, the section dealing with educational context is also the result of specific options and priorities. Chapters dealing with providing educational service and attention to diversity in the CAPV/EAE are intended to provide the readers with a general overview on how the system in general addresses these topics and how various schools demonstrate their commitment to such issues. Likewise, research and experiences that were developed in schools are submitted and analyzed; for example, the socialization program for gender violence prevention; the psycho-educational intervention programs based on cooperative games; and experiences in resolution and transformation of conflicts within the school setting.

The second part of the volume brings together various chapters concerned with a broader view. We have termed this the socio-educational context, because the search for greater levels of equality and fairness is not a matter that concerns only formal education systems in general and schools in particular. Rather, it involves many other social agents, and the successes or failures in terms of the goals stated also depend on the capabilities, commitment and involvement of said agents. The collective nature of those goals also requires collective strategies for momentum and growth. Thus, we must approach the analysis of equality and fairness from a broad perspective, aware that we are facing complex realities that cannot be caught within limited contexts such as schooling alone. Within the socio-educational context, social agents exert a capacity to influence the perceptions, the acquisition of beliefs, and the conduct and behaviors of citizens. On the one hand, the lived social experience in itself puts these citizens in touch with values and experiences that lead to different forms of socialization, integration, identity development, and so on. On the other, within that context there is the possibility of acting in a systematic and deliberate manner through programs with a pedagogical vocation, aimed at developing citizens to be more fully and better integrated socially, and consequently leading to a more fair and balanced society.

Therefore, this text covers in the second section research and experiences relating to socio-educational contexts beyond that of education alone, where the actual and effective involvement of those other agents becomes key in the conception and materialization of essentially educational projects. Specifically, the articles included in this second section deal with the social construction of values through media outlets; the socialization and integration of the immigrant population; the redefinition of the concept of family and contemporary forms of participating from the family in educational processes; and the development of learning communities.

This text shows different approaches to and the means by which equality and fairness are promoted. It is true that societies usually provide answers quite similar to the challenges they share, but unique experiences are a source of learning. And in our immediate milieu, the CAPV/EAE, there is a level of commitment toward the goals mentioned which is reflected in various observations, research and programs. We have brought together some of these in this text, without attempting to reach beyond the goals stated. And these are simply to make available to the readers some of the more significant examples of the activities in connection with the existent educational equality and fairness in the CAPV/EAE.

More than two centuries have elapsed since the educational project of the Enlightenment took shape; two centuries during which education has demonstrated its potential as an engine for integration, and during which time there have been enormous social, economic and cultural changes. However, the validity of that project remains plausible because a very important part of educational activity today still fulfills the same basic goal: social and cultural integration as a mechanism for compensating and contributing to equality and fairness.

This text examines education from this standpoint, situated within a specific context—the Basque Country—and highlights the existence of problems and inequities that expose the complexities of our societies, as well as some educational answers that attempt to mitigate them. Standing alone, these answers are embedded in disparate fields of knowledge and theoretical points of view. By presenting them together, we are able to share and transfer knowledge. Education is a broad concept, always under construction, that must continually adapt to the requirements of social change and human needs.

Part 1

Education in the Basque Country

1

Education Provision in the Basque Country

ALFONSO UNCETA and ANDRÉS DAVILA

The belief that education is a basic asset for the purposes of equal opportunity of individuals and, therefore, for the purposes of lessening social inequities, is entirely linked to the birth and subsequent consolidation of the contemporary liberal state. As Alejandro Álvarez indicated, "the history of contemporary states is also the history of public instruction systems; starting at that point in time educating the people became a strategic matter and its practices became academic" (2001, 40). That is why education was not considered by the Enlightenment as an autonomous entity, but rather as a crucial element within a broader and more general phenomenon of social change, structural in nature, with the state playing the leading role. As pointed out by Antonio Viñao Frago, "the essential defining feature of contemporary educational political thought is the quantitative extension of the educational reality" (1982, 18).

With these ideas in mind, the Enlightenment conceived education within a process of structural social change, with the nation-state taking a leading role as a device or agent serving as catalyst for a change always steered from the position of power and toward the people, consisting in due time of subjects, and later on citizens, in a non-commercial partnership.[1] Therefore the nation-state is the essential sociohistoric agent that served as a driving force of a new concept of education, understood as concrete, institutionalized practices, as a system of instruction.[2]

---

1. See as an example, Barreiro Rodríguez (1987); also Ossenbach and De Puelles (1990).
2. The work of Boli and Ramírez is quite eloquent in this regard (1999, 294–308); likewise Ruiz Berrio (2000).

The materialization of the state's educational project took the school as a central and specific institution, conceived as a public service. The institutionalization of the school was thus linked to an emerging political culture in which the state became the guarantor for the liabilities and rights of the citizenry. In this regard and as pointed out by Eugenio Rodríguez Fuenzalida, "the idea of national public service has been the inspiration in the creation of the national schooling system, oriented and managed from the central state (the state gradually became responsible for the community education that existed in some countries during the mid-nineteenth century), affordable and accessible (education has for a long time been free-of-charge at almost every level), compulsory at the elementary level and with a curricular and structural proposal similar for an entire country" (1994, 54). Thus, under the guidance of the state, schools were at least partially recognized as places for fostering fairness, mainstreaming, and the development and training of citizens.

The perception of education as a public asset to be delivered essentially and almost exclusively by the state underwent a transformation starting with the revisiting of the public service concept. In this sense, the Universal Declaration of Human Rights approved by the UN General Assembly on December 10, 1948 became particularly significant.[3] Its most noteworthy consequence was that as a result of article 26 setting forth not only the public interest of education but also the right to freedom of instruction, the classic connotation that the term *private* carried in educational settings was going to be replaced by the concept of "private activity of public interest." José Gimeno Sacristán accurately expresses this evolution, "from the clear classical contrast between the public school supported by public funds and the private school supported by funds from its direct clients, there is a shift to a milder contrast: all services of interest to the community are deemed public. Public education and private education become alternative means to facilitate the same ends, to be justified in terms of the educational models they serve in a pluralistic society" (1996, 62).

In practice, most of the constitutions and legislatures of European states came to formally acknowledge the right to education and principle of freedom of instruction, even though the effective attainment of both (and therefore the state's commitment to their development) varies greatly depending on which society we are considering. All this has logi-

---

3. See www.un.org/.

cally brought about an intense debate concerning the extent of the state's commitment to private education, or simply whether it is capable of effectively guaranteeing its citizens' rights and educational freedoms.

Thus, from the second half of the twentieth century on, the educational concept of what is private underwent a transformation to the extent that currently, although only in a certain sense, it may not be as easy to clearly differentiate it from what is public, and even less to portray it in terms of opposition to the latter. A new model has been in development, wherein the concept of what is public has lost quite a bit of its richness and meaning, and therefore educational opposition between public and private now appears to be more inconsistent.

Nevertheless, from our point of view, far from being categorized under what has formally been defined as a complementarity relationship, the public-private education alternative has been established in terms of competence amongst different services and educational concepts of a different structure, as is also the case with the social perception concerning both. As Robert Ballion reminds us, "it seems logical to assume that the choice of private instruction is due to a comparison having been established between both sectors, which is equivalent to saying that behind the institutional quasi-similarity of these two systems (same funding, same teaching staff, same tests, same tutorial management...), functional differences exist due to the fact that they do not assure the same type of educational service" (1999, 274).

Thus, the distinction between public and private education is not just legal, but it also results from different ways of understanding concepts such as the mission of education, freedom of instruction, or the right to education, and these different concepts are precisely those that explain the content which in each case various social groups attribute to public and private education.[4] In fact, what is public and what is private constitute categories involving two different spheres that people experience in their daily lives.[5] But from the educational standpoint the relevant issue is that for decades now private schools in the Western world, without relin-

---

4. Here it is worth mentioning an ethnographic study carried out by Díaz de Rada (1996) for several years at two secondary education schools (one public, one private). This study brings to light the differences in daily structure within specific schools, such as, in this case, those between a public (*instituto*) and private (*colegio*) high school in Madrid during the late 1980's and early 1990's.

5. The nature of the relationship between the public and private realms described by modern cultural theorists poses certain peculiarities that differentiate it from a strictly legal percep-

quishing their private nature, are considered providers of a public service and are able to access public funding of their activities.

The Current Educational Setting

As a result of the fact that, as a direct consequence of the successful development of the schooling process, education now enjoys widespread implementation and one of the essential goals of the Enlightment idea of universal schooling is already a reality in advanced societies, the new frame of reference for educational policies is quality. This tends to appear as an absolute and strategic goal that is collective in nature. The term quality includes specific values linked to apparently technical criteria, formally rational in nature, but that are in reality rooted in a multiform concept with multiple possible meanings. In fact, it is difficult to assign the same meaning to the notion of quality when we measure it against different social and educational realities.

So schools or other schools, increasingly installed within the rules of competition and the market, must design specific educational projects that address their capabilities, their goals and the particular features of their social setting. Under such circumstances and although in a different order of priorities and intensity, developments in thinking about quality have included in their analyses not only an observation of the essential components of the school (the faculty, the student body and in no small part the parents), but also in terms of the tools inherent in the emerging model (planning, assessment, administrative management, involvement, counseling, autonomy, and so forth) and finally in reference to the determination of quality indicators (financial, social, staff-oriented, results-oriented, and so forth).

Taking a position with regards to these variables is essential for the purposes of defining the quality model one assumes. Thus, quality as a goal in its practical application gives rise to a new setting that is very directly related to concerns about educational service and the relationships between public and private education. In this regard, Carlos Lerena well reminds us that "public and private instruction have essentially different audiences, a different clientele: audiences and customers of a different social caliber in a different position and with a different rela-

---

tion of both. Among others, on this relationship see S.N. Eisenstadt (1973); Apter (1965); and Berger, Berger and Kellner (1973).

tionship established within academic culture. This is an essential part of what is remarkably hidden when talking about quality of instruction" (1986, 342).

These comments indicate that the goals of quality are neither standardized nor can they be invoked from a standpoint outside the benchmark social setting, as a constraint on the educational activity. Avoidance of such evidence is equivalent to denying the specific interrelationship between school and society and failing to recognize that educational quality—and the forms it adopts—should be evaluated within the framework of that relationship. Otherwise any analysis would be similar to disregarding the close relationship that exists between the levels of academic success and the social, economic and cultural status of the student body. This is emphasized by Bert Creemers: "The quality of a school is the average score on an output measure corrected for input characteristics, thereby indicating the 'value added' by the school. Equity refers to the compensatory power of schools. Some schools are more successful in compensating for the input characteristics of students (social class, gender, ethnic background and prior achievement) than others. Depending on the dimension of effectiveness, the output of schools can be judged according to the concepts of quality and equity" (1996, 23).

Undoubtedly it appears that the non-school setting has a major impact on the frame of mind and academic achievement of the student body. Socioeconomic background, cultural and social skills, and the family structure and situation, are some of the factors that facilitate or complicate educational development and academic success. Therefore, any concept of quality that fails to recognize these realities will be avoiding all those factors that produce inequities and increase the diversity of the student body.

Bearing all this in mind, the purpose of the complaints aimed at education, demanding compensation and redistribution, is to mitigate the individual and contextual differences present in our societies. Thus, education considered as a public service implies that schools financed with public funds must respond to those complaints, regardless of whether they are public of private. Given this, it is evident that the type of students taught at a school, their characteristics and social composition, represent crucial elements in the development of the educational mission. And only by considering these issues is it appropriate to think about the concept of quality, its content, and goals in each specific case.

In addition, what often happens with students from disadvantaged socioeconomic backgrounds is that their situation worsens if the schooling takes place in a low-ranked school in terms of structure and background. And obviously the actual possibilities in the schools delivering instruction to this type of students are also quite limited. Thus, as indicated by Álvaro Marchesi:

> the delivery of equitable education to students then becomes a growing demand from broad segments of the educational community, particulary those commited to defending public instruction, and is viewed with misgivings by those other segments defending freedom of school choice on the part of families, more closely linked with state-subsidized and private instruction. It is a matter of extraordinary importance for the harmonious operation of the educational system and also to prevent certain schools from being overwhelmed by the number of students with learning difficulties who must be taught. (2004, 247)

It may be assumed from the foregoing that in societies such as ours, where education is deemed a public service and is therefore financed with public funds, the goals assigned to education should pertain equally to all schools financed with public funds, regardless of their type of ownership. Therefore, the pursuit of quality in delivering educational service means that schools as a whole should reflect the necessary balance between efficiency and fairness. But the fact is that quality, efficiency and fairness are concepts that carry meanings and significance with differing or diverging interpretations.

This possibly explains why the reality is full of examples showing considerable differences amongst the schools: differences in ownership, location, student body, resources, social settings, services provided, social image, and so on. Evidence of such numerous and at times so essential differences demonstrates the lack of balance in delivering educational services. This imbalance becomes particularly obvious when comparing the contribution of public and subsidized-private schools[6] to educational equality and fairness.

---

6. Subsidized-private schools are those financed with public funds. They are termed *concertados* because they participate in *concert* with the regulations in the judicial/financial instrument as provided by the government in order to assign public funds to the rendering of education as a public service.

This circumstance has much to do with the fact that education has always represented a mechanism for social distinction; something that is true for those who had access to schooling while others did not. This is also true for those who made progress in educational rankings while others could not. And it was always true for those who were able to obtain an education for a price, undoubtedly the feature that best defines the value of a product. Therefore, those who acquire quality products are socially recognized, in detriment to other products and other producers. And the acquisition of good products requires certain conditions. However, said conditions are not usually too compatible with other goals more appropriate to the educational task, such as contributing to equality and fairness.

Using the above comments as starting point, our purpose is to analyze to what extent schools are commited to fulfilling their social mission. The assumption we would like to argue is the equality and balance between public schools and subsidized-private schools, each financed with public funds. And we intend to analyze this matter in the case of the Comunidad Autónoma del País Vasco/Euskal Autonomia Erkidegoa (CAPV/EAE, Autonomous Community of the Basque Country), which, as we have already stated elsewhere (Unceta and Aguirre, 2001), has several special features when compared to other educational systems within the European setting.

The Academic Uniqueness of the CAPV/EAE

Since October 30, 1980, the CAPV/EAE government, has full decision-making authority in non-university education, in compliance with the Statute of Autonomy of the Basque Country.[7] In addition to other unique features we will not discuss here,[8] the CAPV/EAE educational system has as a very special dimension the strong implementation of private instruction, and particularly the diversity in ownership of the schools involved. Likewise in the CAPV/EAE, funding of education in general and of sub-

---

7. The Basque Country enjoys a broad level of autonomy by virtue of the Statute of Autonomy of the Basque Country, approved on December 18, 1979. This results from the Spanish Constitution of 1977 wherein Spain became a state of autonomies and where the autonomy statutes became the basic institutional norm that regulates the jurisdictional relationships between each autonomous community and the state.

8. Bilingualism and the specific importance of career or vocational training are two of its more relevant features. A description of the CAPV/EAE educational system can be found in Unceta (2001).

sidized-private education in particular is much greater than that of Spain as a whole at present.

In terms of the schools offering subsidized-private education, they basically belong to three different types of ownership: the Church; the ikastola movement; and cooperative schools.

Religious schools belonging to the Catholic Church represent more than half of the private educational sector. The strength of the Church in the evolution of education in the Basque Country is explained through deep historical roots. As Jesús Arpal et al well point out, "in practice—and in rural areas during the nineteenth century—the man of God, whether or not ordained, was the one in charge of initiating the first words which were the catechism, at a school jointly kept between the church and the council" (Arpal, Asúa and Dávila 1982, 25). Moreover, as we shall explain, the form in which the Church has been active in the world of education in the Basque Country has evolved in terms of political and cultural events.

The first major expansion of these religious schools took place during the second half of the nineteenth century, at the time when religious orders were banished from France. This gave rise to a massive influx of religious congregations arriving in the Basque Country. From this point on, and as aptly pointed out by Maitane Ostolaza, "the Church, sheltered by the compliance agreement between the state and the Church, and by the 1876 Constitution—as a result of the compromise between ecclesiastical and civil powers—would be able to increase without limit its holdings and launch its recatholicizing offensive with the goal of conquering broad social sectors. The privileged means for carrying out its ministry would be found in secondary education, where it would achieve a practically uncontested quasi-monopoly up until the Second Republic [1931]" (2000, 200).

Although during the second half of the twentieth century the Church would partly relinquish its status of absolute leadership in the field of private education, religious educational schools have been able to construct a private setting with the intention of making their niche as one of the academic alternatives to the state's concept of what is public.

Ikastolas are a type of school developed in the Basque Country during the 1960s, as an educational and also identity and cultural reality, which resulted in fostering innovative relationships between those three parameters. To try to understand this model of schooling, it is best to turn to the definition of its origin and purposes by the actual Federation of Ikastolas:

The ikastolas were created from grassroots initiatives, because the academic setting (private as well as public) existing at the time did not satisfy the needs and demands of an important segment of Basque individuals, groups and the community as a whole, who considered the Basque language Euskara as basic core of their identity. School then was an instrument for acculturation and colonization. Across from it the ikastola was born as an academic alternative, with an educational program that took on the features that basically define a people's existence, such as language and culture (Eukal Herriko Ikastolen Elkartea 1988, 7).

In addition to their commitment to teach exclusively in the Basque language, an indicator of the ikastolas' grassroots sense of mission as one of their permanent features, is the fact that since the late 1970s the great majority of them have been regarded as private schools. However, socially as well as in rule-setting the ikastola seeks to prevail as a unique and alternative school, overcoming the traditional distinction between public and private schools. In addition to being a present and future reality that represents approximately 20 percent of the private education sector in the CAPV/EAE, ikastolas have historically been a place for experimenting with organizational and pedagogical forms and defining new operational models. This is one of the issues that most strongly reinforces the public interest of this school model as the bearer of a new system of regulations, pedagogical procedures and cultural contents.[9]

Cooperative schools are made up of groups of individuals who started in grassroots initiatives and who were later recognized as peers in the realms of participation and management. It is a well-known fact that the cooperative tradition in the Basque Country underwent extraordinary growth during the second half of the twentieth century, led by the Mondragón Cooperative Movement , which undoubtedly explains the proliferation of cooperative enterprises in the Basque Country. It is significant that, due to their composition and features, these types of schools usually convey a high degree of commitment toward the educational needs of their surroundings, in which they are often fully anchored. Cooperative schools represent approximately 20 percent of the private education sector in the Basque Country and form a network of quite widespread schools there.

---

9. For greater detail on what an ikastola is and what it represents, see Arrien (1992) and Lasa (1971).

Taking this overview as a starting point in examining private education in the CAPV/EAE, we see that over 50 percent of the student body is schooled in these subsidized-private schools, although this overall percentage may vary depending on the educational phase under consideration, as demonstrated in table 1.1.

Table 1.1. Student body distribution
by educational systems, academic year 2009–10

	Public	Private
Early childhood education	51.2%	48.8%
Primary education	49.8%	50.2%
Compulsory secondary education	45.2%	54.8%
Lower postsecondary	52.7%	47.3%
Vocational schools	55.8%	44.2%

Source: Departament of Education, Universities and Research, Basque Government.

According to the data in table 1.1, there is a more or less even distribution of students between the two educational systems. Therefore, considering the fact that the Basque educational service as a whole is financed by public funds a simple balance based on the equitable mathematical distribution of the student body between the two educational systems, public and private should be pursued. The balance and proportional equality base on fairness should favor the fact that public education and subsidized-private education, beyond their logical specifications, should be educational spaces that can be interchangeably traversed by the diversity of students currently in the Basque educational system.

Nevertheless, the above hypothesis can only be validated or rebutted by analyzing a set of indicators that provide us with significant information on the contribution to fairness originating in public and private education, in terms of supply, student body composition, attention to diversity, and so on. And in view of such indicators, here we seek to describe the differences and similarities among the Basque schools in relation to their supply of educational service.

Delivering Educational Service in the CAPV/EAE: Balance Indicators

Any attempt to analyze how the delivery of educational service in the CAPV/EAE takes place must involve a multidimensional perspective.

Beyond the specific effect of a given indicator, the relationship and interaction between a set of representative indicators is also relevant. Therefore, we have selected five different dimensions that we have assigned a high explanatory value, and that can provide a quite accurate view of the issue we are dealing with. Most of them relate to factors strictly linked to the student body, although ultimately they provide us with a perspective on both types of schools, the places where said factors interact.

Territorial Supply Distribution

In our understanding, the territorial distribution of the educational supply is a distributive indicator directly related to the delivery of educational service, in the sense that it can facilitate or complicate the conditions for access to education by the population as a whole, regardless of their location in the territory. In the case of the CAPV/EAE, the population distribution covers 251 municipalities of varying size and importance. Also, a good part of the population, although of little quantitative significance, is located in small- and medium-sized municipalities, oftentimes some distance away from large communities.

Taking these features into account, how the educational supply is distributed throughout the territory can facilitate or complicate the conditions for access to education for the citizenry as a whole. In the CAPV/EAE, the public supply reaches 76 percent of municipalities and is obviously much more widespread than its subsidized-private counterpart. Particularly significant is the fact that in 117 municipalities in the Basque Country the public supply is exclusive, of 197 total municipalities with educational supply. They are small- and medium-sized municipalities that can thus benefit from schooling under conditions of proximity; this is particularly important during the initial levels of the educational system, when students absolutely depend on their families.

However, the situation changes considerably when we examine the educational supply distribution at the secondary level, which affects students starting at age twelve. In this case, the absolute and relative strength of subsidized-private schools is quite important, and the differences are much less significant. Two causes explain this different setup. Initially, it is due to the fact that during the Franco era private (and mainly religious) schools developed their particular model of academic specialization. Thus, while public schools essentially addressed the demand at the initial stages, private schools underwent a large-scale development in the secondary education sphere, an educational supply that at that time was essentially oriented towards the middle and upper classes. Then there is also the fact that the private supply has had a solid presence in urban communities and metropolitan areas, precisely those places where the demand for secondary education is higher.

Guidelines for Schooling of Foreign Students

Catering for the foreign immigrant population is one of the greatest challenges faced by the Basque educational system today, due to several interrelated factors. First, it is a community that has grown six-fold in the past decade since 2000, increasing its relative weight at different rates on schools. Secondly, the overwhelming majority of these students are from families originating in Latin America and Africa, while those from the European Union or North America are minimally represented. Thirdly, most of these students come from disadvantaged backgrounds, with a low social and cultural level, and usually have scarce financial resources. Fourthly, the lack of knowledge of the two official languages of the CAPV/EAE by a considerable number of immigrants poses an additional difficulty that delays the process of mainstreaming, and adds learning problems.

This set of features has brought the immigrant population to the special attention education authorities. Therefore, the schooling of these communities is addressed through specific procedures in terms of planning and counseling, and a considerable number of material and personal resources have been devoted to these procedures. However, as we shall demonstrate, these students are not evenly distributed among all the schools supported by public funds and instead, considerable differences can be seen in terms of how one and the other educational system contribute to the process of receiving and integrating these students.

In fact, seven out of every ten immigrant students are schooled in the public system, although this overall percentage shows variation in the different territories of the CAPV/EAE.[10] Beyond these territorial differences, it is interesting to note the different contributions of the various educational systems, which is also obviously reflected in the school composition.

---

10. The CAPV/EAE consists of the territories of Araba, Bizkaia, and Gipuzkoa, which are administrative units that also have their own territorial government. Nevertheless, educational responsibilities are handled exclusively by the Basque Government. In 2009, the total population for each different territory was as follows: Araba: 309,786; Bizkaia: 1,144,420; Gipuzkoa: 693,540. For that same year, the population of the CAPV/EAE as a whole was 2,147,754.

Students with Special Educational Needs

Probably one of the most evolved issues within our academic setting is the concept of Special Educational Needs (SEN). The traditional idea of SEN was focused on students bearing some sensory or physical handicap, and the educational response to these communities was guided by their joining specific schools, also known as special schools. Universal access to schooling, by definitely increasing student diversity, has redefined the concept of SEN; so it is from the diversity standpoint—be it physical, linguistic, economic or social—that the existence of an educational need is defined and assessed; an educational need which is also designed not only from a personal but also from a social dimension. Further, a decisive and unequivocal commitment has been made toward inclusion and academic mainstreaming, with responses generating from regular schools.

Currently, in most cases responses are introduced in regular classrooms and result from an increase in academic resources to support group efforts, the design of alternative learning situations, or providing specific students with a more personalized attention and in particular groups, as part of their school day. These are known as special education or support groups, and are an indicator of the resources and attention schools devote to diversity, in an attempt to offer greater quality and fairness in education.

Table 1.2. Percentage of special education (SE) classes as compared to total early childhood and elementary classes, by territory and school type, academic year 2009–10

	Public			Private			All schools		
	SE classes	Total classes	%	SE classes	Total classes	%	SE classes	Total classes	%
Araba	85	780	11%	24	469	5%	109	1249	9%
Bizkaia	285	2417	12%	117	1948	6%	402	4365	9%
Gipuzkoa	149	1585	9%	81	1396	6%	230	2981	8%
CAPV/EAE	519	4782	11%	222	3813	6%	741	8595	9%

Source: Department of Education, Universities and Research, Basque Government.

Table 1.2 demonstrates that currently and at the initial stages of the educational system in the CAPV/EAE (ages three to twelve), 9 percent of operating classrooms are regarded as special classrooms where alternative learning methods and processes are developed. As can be seen, 70 percent of these special groups are located in public schools, and the relative involvement of subsidized-private schools is in all instances below the CAPV/EAE average.

The breakdown is significantly more balanced at the compulsory secondary education level (ages twelve to sixteen). At this stage the attention to diversity is particularly complex, taking into account age, frame of mind, and features of a part of the student body. Furthermore, it must be noted that this stage is the final stretch of compulsory education where the private system teaches 10 percent more students than its public counterpart. Notwithstanding this quantitative difference, 55 percent of special or support classrooms are located in public schools, although in fact at this stage the involvement of subsidized-private schools is greater in terms of attention to diversity. While at the early childhood and elementary education levels 6 percent of active groups in the subsidized-private schools are special or support classrooms, at the compulsory secondary education level the percentage of this type of classrooms is double.

The information contained in tables 1.2 and 1.3 is extremely relevant because these types of resources lead to many of the conditions that help schools become truly inclusive and respond to the growing diversity of the student body, which becomes markedly so as the students' age increases.

Table 1.3. Special education (SE) classes compared to total secondary classes, by territory and school type, academic year 2009–10

	Public			Private			All centers		
	SE classes	Total secondary	%	SE classes	Total secondary	%	SE classes	Total secondary	%
Araba	42	254	17%	30	259	12%	72	513	14%
Bizkaia	142	885	16%	110	878	13%	252	1763	14%
Gipuzkoa	78	588	13%	73	606	12%	151	1194	13%
CAPV/EAE	262	1727	15%	213	1743	12%	475	3470	14%

Source: Department of Education, Universities and Research, Basque Government.

Socioeconomic Background and Students' Schooling

Within the European context numerous studies[11] attribute a good portion of the inequities experienced by students in their school years to their socioeconomic backgrounds. This appears to be a particularly determining factor of scholastic performance in the case of students from low or specifically disadvantaged backgrounds. This consideration of an individual nature needs to be also stated with regards to another contextual variable, to wit, the composition and socioeconomic context of the schools themselves. In connection with this, Alvaro Marchesi recalls that "students with greater scholastic underdevelopment due to their poor socioeconomic background will see their situation worsen if they are being schooled in a school that also reflects a low average performance. A low personal socioeconomic background together with a school's low average performance is a potentially dangerous combination" (2004, 46). It should be noted that socioeconomic level as a variable is difficult to measure, since it usually results from a set of indicators. A good indicator, however, is the number of students on scholarship, and it has been found six out of every ten students on scholarship are schooled in public schools. Moreover, it is worth noting that 75 percent of the schools with more than 40 percent of students on scholarship are public, and that this rises to 81 percent in the case of schools with more than 60 percent students on scholarship. Obviously this makeup again establishes limitations on the development of the educational mission in many schools.

When considering the matter from the standpoint of the individual, in other words, if we look at the number of students on scholarship being schooled under each educational system, we also see important differences (as shown in table 1.4). At either educational level, the public system is the recipient of a much greater number of students on scholarship, and this overall imbalance is more pronounced in the realm of compulsory education.

---

11. Especially valuable are the Pisa Reports (Programme for International Student Assessment) that measure the abilities of students from different countries in different areas of knowledge within the European setting. The Pisa Report 2000 dealt with reading competency; the Pisa Report 2003 was on mathematical capabilities; Pisa Report 2006 involved abilities in the natural sciences; and Pisa Report 2009 measured students' abilities in the digital era. They are available at www.oecd.org/.

Table 1.4. Percentage of scholarship students in compulsory education (ages 3–16), and in overall educational system (ages 3–19) by systems, academic year 2008–9.

System	% on scholarship compulsory	% on scholarship overall
Public	50.3%	44.3%
Private	30.6%	28.6%

Source: Department of Education, Universities and Research, Basque Government.

Educational Systems and Students' Qualifications

The lack of coincidence between the students' actual age and the theoretical age for the academic level in which they are enrolled is an indicator of academic delay, because the lack of appropriateness in terms of students' age points to a lesser probability of academic success; it also reflects a factual delay in academic advancement, and finally, it becomes one of the reasons for the early drop-out rate in a good number of students.

Table 1.5. Distribution of inappropriate-aged students between academic systems and educational levels, academic years 2005–6 through 2008–9

Educational Levels	2005–6		2006–7		2007–8		2008–9	
	Public	Private	Public	Private	Public	Private	Public	Private
Elementary	60.5	39.5	61.1	38.9	62.7	37.3	65.5	34.5
Secondary	53.8	46.2	54.8	45.2	55.0	45.0	55.5	44.5
Post-secondary	61.6	38.4	60.3	39.7	60.3	39.7	59.2	40.8
Total	57.0	43.0	57.4	42.6	57.9	42.1	58.7	41.3

Source: Department of Education, Universities and Research, Basque Government.

In the case of the CAPV/EAE educational system, the lack of appropriateness is more pronounced in public schools than in subsidized-private schools, as shown in table 1.5. This brings about various consequences on the development of the educational task. From an individual standpoint, students of an inappropriate age are usually one of the groups with worse academic results; in addition to their difficulties in adaptation they at times develop social interaction problems, and in a large number of cases disrupt the actual dynamics of the educational activities. From the group standpoint, treating this type of students forces the faculty to develop specific strategies aimed at mainstreaming them into the classroom.

The faculty assigns a great deal of importance to this indicator, because a significant presence of a particular group of what is colloquially known as "repeaters"[12] is a factor that distorts the group dynamics, may disrupt social interaction, and end up affecting the potentials and results of the group itself.

Concluding Comments from the Educational Fairness Standpoint

The contribution to equality and fairness can also be analyzed by taking into account other indicators that are different from those we have suggested in these comments. Moreover, we are aware that the manner of approaching this topic also varies in terms of the educational, social and ideological point of view guiding the analysis. But it is an undeniable fact that equality and fairness must necessarily be linked to the appropriate educational requirements of each historical era.

In this regard, a series of features exist today that cannot be ignored when trying to specify what should be the contribution to educational equality and fairness. Regardless of the point of view employed in analyzing the current educational reality, this reality clashes inevitably with the problems of heterogeneity and diversity, social, cultural and economic differences, and other inequities of a different nature. These are all problems that the students themselves represent and bring forth into the school setting.

It seems obvious that the delivery of educational service should try to short-cut this set of problems beyond the different public or private nature of schools. And if both versions of educational service develop under identical settings, the principle of equal distribution should be the benchmark. However, the mathematical balance typical in the distribution of the student body between public education and subsidized-private education in the Basque Country breaks up when considering the features of students schooled under one system and the other.

---

12. This term describes those students who, having failed to attain the necessary passing results, must repeat the same academic level.

This unequal distribution is particularly relevant at a time when states have been promoting the goal of quality as one of the priorities in the educational systems. This is a goal that must be developed by the schools, and we have seen how they differ depending on quite varied circumstances. Thus, quality becomes a matter of scales. In other words, the topic of discussion should instead be *qualities*, different levels of quality for different types of schools involved in schooling various types of students.

Finally, the goals linked to quality and fairness can take the students as units of analysis, as well as schools, but only the broadest point of view actually informs us on how an education system contributes to their development. And in the case of the educational system of the CAPV/ EAE, the delivery of educational service accounts for significant imbalances, particularly relating to the contribution by one educational system and the other. This is because in view of the information available, and faced with the concept that public and private education are two similar settings in the delivery of educational service, reality highlights their crucial differences.

References

Álvarez, Alejandro. 2001. "Del Estado docente a la sociedad educadora: ¿Un cambio de época?" *Revista Iberoamericana de Educación* 26 (May–August): 35–58.

Apter, David E. 1965. *The Politics of Modernization*. Chicago: University of Chicago Press.

Arpal, Jesús, Begoña Asúa, and Paul Dávila. 1982. *Educación y Sociedad en el País Vasco*. Donostia-San Sebastián: Txertoa.

Arrien, Gregorio. 1992. Bizkaiako Ikastolak 1957–1972. Beren hasiera eta antolaketa. Donostia: Eusko Ikaskuntza.

Ballion, Robert. 1999. "La enseñanza privada, ¿una escuela a medida?" In *Sociología de la Educación. Lecturas básicas y textos de apoyo*, edited by Mariano Fernández Enguita. Barcelona: Ariel.

Barreiro Rodríguez, Herminio. 1987. "La educación como cuestión de Estado: de Platón a la Ilustración francesa." *Historia de la Educación* 6: 161–69.

Berger, Peter, Briggitte Berger, and Hansfried Kellner. 1973. *The Homeless Mind: Modernization and Consciousness*. New York: Random House.

Boli, John, and Francisco Ramírez. 1999. "La construcción política de la escolarización de masas: sus orígenes europeos y escolarización mundial." In *Sociología de la Educación. Lecturas básicas y textos de apoyo*, edited by Mariano Fernández Enguita. Barcelona: Ariel.

Creemers, Bert. 1996. "The School Effectiveness Knowledge Base." In David Reynolds, Robert Bollen, Bert Creemers, David Hopkins, Louise Stoll and Nijs Lagerweij. *Making Good Schools: Linking School Effectiveness and School Improvement*. London: Routledge.

Díaz de Rada, Ángel. 1996. Los primeros de la clase y los últimos románticos. Una etnografía para la crítica de la visión instrumental de la enseñanza. Madrid: Siglo XXI.

Eisenstadt, S.N. 1973. *Tradition, Change, and Modernity*. New York: Wiley.

Euskal Herriko Ikastolen Elkartea. 1988. *La Ikastola. Carácter y Estructura*. Zarautz: Euskal Herriko Ikastolen Elkartea.

Gimeno Sacristán, José. 1996. "Los retos de la educación pública. Cómo lo necesario puede devenir en desfasado." *Cuadernos de Pedagogía* 248 (June): 59–67.

Lasa, José. 1971. *Euskal Erria eta Ikastola. Una polémica en torno a la ikastola*. Donostia: Edili.

Lerena, Carlos. 1986. "Enseñanza pública y privada en España: sobre el porvenir de una ilusión." In *Marxismo y Sociología de la Educación*, edited by Mariano Fernández Enguita. Madrid: Akal.

Marchesi, Álvaro. 2004. *Qué será de nosotros los malos alumnos*. Madrid: Alianza Editorial.

Ossenbach, Gabriela, and Manuel De Puelles. 1990. *La revolución francesa y su influencia en la educación en España*. Madrid: UNED.

Ostolaza, Maitane. 2000. *Entre Religión y Modernidad: Los colegios de las Congregaciones religiosas en la construcción de la sociedad guipuzcoana contemporánea, 1876–1931*. Bilbao: UPV/EHU.

Reynolds, David, Robert Bollen, Bert Creemers, David Hopkins, Louise Stoll, and Nijs Lagerweij. 1996. *Making Good Schools: Linking School Effectiveness and School Improvement*. London: Routledge.

Rodríguez Fuenzalida, Eugenio. 1994. "Criterios de análisis de la calidad en el sistema escolar y sus dimensiones." *Revista Iberoamericana de Educación* 5 (May–August): 45–65.

Ruiz Berrio, Julio, ed. 2000. *La cultura escolar de Europa: Tendencias históricas emergentes.* Madrid: Biblioteca Nueva.

Unceta, Alfonso. 2001. "Procesos fundamentales del sistema educativo no universitario del País Vasco." *Inguruak, Revista de Sociología y Ciencia Política* 30 (September): 39–65.

Unceta, Alfonso, and Nekane Aguirre. 2001. "Aproximación a las dimensiones público y privado en el sistema educativo no universitario de la CAPV." *Revista Vasca de Administración Pública* 61, no. 2 (September–December): 15–52.

Viñao Frago, Antonio. 1982. *Política y educación en los orígenes de la España contemporánea: Examen especial de sus relaciones en la enseñanza secundaria.* Madrid: Siglo XXI.

2

Addressing Basque Diversity in the Classroom: Measures to Avoid Excluding At-Risk Youth

BEGOÑA MARTÍNEZ DOMÍNGUEZ

The discourse on addressing diversity issues in a unique and comprehensive educational system in the Comunidad Autónoma del País Vasco/ Euskal Autonomia Erkidegoa (CAPV/EAE, Autonomous Community of the Basque Country) was pioneered in 1982, on the basis of the *Plan de Educación Especial para El País Vasco* (Special education plan for the Basque Country; Department of Education, Universities and Research 1982), through the process of integrating individuals who were then considered markedly different ("special"), into regular schools.

Since then, the proposed goal of "Building a school with room for all children in Euskadi (the Basque Country)," continues to be the greatest challenge faced by the educational system and society in general. And while this discourse continues to influence dominant academic and social decision-making and the two educational system reforms (LOGSE and LOE[1]), the necessary covergences that once emphasized *integration* have evolved into what is known today as the *inclusive school* (Martínez 2002; Orcasitas 2005).

The CAPV/EAE educational administration has recently developed various measures aimed at addressing diversity issues. By gradually applying these measures (*regular, specific,* and *exceptional*) the intent is to educate those students who for various reasons—particularly in compulsory

---

1. Statutory Education Act (*Ley Orgánica de Educación* [Constitutional Law on Education] LOE), of May 3, 2006, published in the BOE on May 4, 2006.

secondary education[2] —find it difficult to maintain regular learning processes. However, assessments of the efficiency of these methods are scarce and seldom public.

Therefore, our research began with the implementation of the first "extreme" measure at the secondary level (ages twelve through sixteen). Our primary goal was to ascertain whether the implementation of these measures improved the quality of inclusive teaching; or if these measures served as a useful smoke screen to create parallel and lesser-valued educational paths for the most vulnerable children and adolescents.

We present our research in three main sections. First, we discuss the basic details typical of the social exclusion focus, this being the overall framework our studies are based on. Second, we describe our various research projects and report on the measures analyzed. We then conclude with a summary synthesis of our most recent study and some general findings.

The Educational Exclusion Perspective

Given the abundance of parameters, relationships, and forces linked to "addressing diversity issues" as a formula for preventing failure in a comprehensive teaching model, it is difficult to find a theoretical framework to describe them all.

Nor is it easy to establish satisfactory connections between available knowledge and consistent practices and policies, since they—as well as equity policies—need to be submitted to more careful and critical study (Popkewitz and Lindblad 2007). In other studies (Martínez 2005; Escudero 2005) we propose that—in addition to a discussion on modes of thinking, defining, and taking action—there was a need to incorporate into the diversity discourse certain unavoidable ethical principles that would make it possible to connect the right to being different with the struggle against educational exclusion, as well as with social justice and democratic growth.

In any case, and recognizing that it is missing key elements, we believe that Edward Sellman's organic views (2009), and the personal, professional, institutional, and contextual inquiry strategies provided by research into social exclusion, provide an appropriate critical lense through which to

---

2. This is what is termed *Educación Secundario Obligatoria* (ESO) or compulsory secondary education.

approach diversity and its hidden face—academic failure suffered within educational systems by the "most different" and vulnerable individuals.

Social exclusion studies give rise to an abundant and widespread field of knowledge surrounding the understanding of old and new forms of exclusion—educational exclusion being one of them—within the structures and processes of social, political, cultural and economic transformation that are specific to neoliberal capitalism and information society (Sen and Klinsberg 2008; Castel 2004; Luengo 2007). Following the outline employed by Juan Manuel Escudero, Mª Teresa González, and Begoña Martínez (2009) we below indicate certain key elements of this approach.

Defining Exclusion

In terms of compulsory education, exclusion occurs in those situations where certain students are deprived of essential elements of learning or appropriate opportunities to learn. The basic competencies framework of the European Union and undertaken by the current educational reform in Spain (LOE) hopes to implement certain learning elements that compulsory education should guarantee to all individuals by means of ethical, justice, and fairness considerations.

Schooling and the Exclusion and Inclusion Trajectory

Social exclusion (Subirats 2004; Tezanos 2001) should be understood as a continuum between two extreme situations: inclusion and exclusion. Its evolution can reflect different levels of intensity and coverage. There could be drastic, strong, final, and unappealable exclusions, and others that are more subtle, extenuated, or partial. Likewise the word *vulnerability* is used, or *risk of exclusion*, to designate intermediate areas between those two theoretical extreme points of exclusion and inclusion. However, when personalizing this continuum, it is common to talk about students in risk areas, or vulnerable students. This implies falling back on categories that can become "labels" with potentially harmful consequences.

Moreover, learning involves elements that are not static, but unique phenomena in process. That is why it is so important to understand that schooling for any student is symbolically a journey, with intermediate stages linked to the past, in process of execution in different forms of the present, open or closed toward the future, where processes of social exclusion and/or learning can take place (Martínez 2004). Therefore, this process focus demands acute awareness of the gradual detachment from school, the gestation of indifference, and the cumulative academic difficulties we detect in an increasingly greater percentage of the students, who are reaching the end of their studies without the essential training or credentials. It would be preferable to talk less about failure in the abstract, and more about life histories of failure or overcoming its threats (Bolívar and Gijón 2008; Parrilla, Gallego, and Moriña 2009), specially having seen that the process of discussion, describing paths and creating narratives helps in the struggle against fate and in disengaging that halo of mystery that self-fulfilling academic prophecies often acquire (Supinos 2009).

New Labels and Exclusions as a Result of the Neutral Term "Diversity"

Inclusion and exclusion are two sides of the same coin. They are born and nurtured through discourse and rationalizations, and also by the specific historical and changing but effective complex interplay between given structures, relationships, and forces that pull together and at the same time pull apart.

Exclusion phenomena are incomprehensible unless consideration is given to the relationship they bear with a given rational order, which is neither arbitrary nor accidental, but linked and triggerred by the social, economic, and cultural system that generates it, as well as the powers and interests it defends. Therefore, without certain particular social orders such as those currently in effect, there would be no exclusion, or it would not exist in the form we currently know it or have known it in the past.

On a similar note, when analyzing failure and the steps taken when attempting to overcome it, they clearly bear a close relationship with a particular academic order that in itself is related to the dominant discourses, which in turn are used to subject students to new forms of labeling and classifying, as well as to a system of duties and responsibilities whereby failure is attributed to individuals "incapable" of succeeding, due to various reasons: social ranking, ethnic group, migrant status, "subject for reinforcement," "for support," and so on.

Some Measures Designed for Integration Can Constitute Subtle Forms of Exclusion

Democratic school systems such as the CAPV/EAE's theoretically guarantee access to all individuals and stability in the compulsory stage. These systems demonstrate their good intentions by "including" those students who have been classified as "not adapted" to the regular setting in special plans and programs. This type of inclusion serves to alleviate or reduce severe inbalances, but the risk exists that these practices result in approving some or other forms of incomplete or unfavorable inclusion. If to this we add the fact that the boundaries for a legitimate inclusion not only cut across the school, but are also created and nurtured outside of the school (defined by a social, family, environmental, and neighborhood order, or perhaps a lack of order) then the risk of extending and intensifying exclusion is even greater.

Researching Diversity Issues in the CAPV/EAE

When the process of integrating individuals with special needs in all regular schools first began in the CAPV/EAE, our team at the Universidad del País Vasco/Euskal Herriko Unibertsitatea (UPV/EHU, University of the Basque Country) shared the responsibility for the initial training of professionals, who up until then had been involved only with students deemed "special." We were charged with the tasking of training nonspecialized professionals as support faculty. This provided the opportunity to research the change in mindsets and practices involved in the transition from an intervention model based on deficiency, to one of *diversity inclusion*.

Studies Performed

Our research began during the 1995–1996 academic year, with a study of the new profile and training of support faculty in compulsory education. This study involved the cooperation of the thirty-five professionals who participated in the training. Aided by questionnaires, interviews, discussion groups, and the tracking and analysis of journals and written accounts in connection with the training courses, a training and support model was designed more in tune with the approach toward diversity provided for in the LOGSE (Pérez-Sostoa and Martínez 1996; Martínez 2001). This has been a benchmark in subsequent training for the various support professionals (Galarreta, Martínez, Orcasitas, and Pérez-Sostoa 1999).

For the second and third projects, research focused on putting curricular diversification programs into practice. The first step addressing diversity issues was initiated at secondary schools in the CAPV/EAE. By means of interviews and questionnaires directed to 3 administrators, 25 management teams, 20 guidance counselors, 95 teachers (classified according to fields, specific groups, and regular groups), and 280 students, we learned what ratings all the individuals involved assigned to these programs. Upon graduation by the first class from the secondary schools in compliance with this measure, the second project was carried out in order to analyze the development and rating of diversification programs, taking as the basic unit of analysis twenty-five representative schools. The results are evidence of the institutional impact resulting from the implementation of this measure (Galarreta, Martínez, Orcasitas, and Pérez-Sostoa 2000).

During academic years from 2003 to 2005, with the secondary education reform having been completed, the fourth project was performed, analyzing the response to diversity measures in secondary schools. This project analyzed the specific measures adopted in the CAPV/EAE. This time we were able to compile opinions from administrators, inspectors, and other external support services by means of interviews. There was also cooperation from administrators at ninety-five secondary schools. The results highlighted the organizational and curricular complexity involved, in terms of the schools dealing with all the measures being applied: electiveness, reinforcement, individual curricular adaptation, a specific educational intervention project, a curricular diversification program, and a supplementary schooling program. The study also took into account the ambivalence these measures created in the development of the inclusive school (Galarreta, Martínez, Mendizabal, Orcasitas, and Pérez-Sostoa 2003; Galarreta, Martínez, Orcasitas, and Pérez-Sostoa 2006).

The uncertainty of the results obtained and the understanding that the last measure—supplementary programs—were being developed outside of regular schools, gave rise to the need to go beyond the regular curriculum and analyze in greater depth the most extreme and palliative measures. This resulted in two projects that took place during the 2007 and 2008 academic years, "Continuous training, encouraging entrepreneurship, and youth at risk of exclusion" and "Experiences and good training practices in professional initiation with youth at risk of exclusion," which we will discuss later on (Martínez, Pérez-Sostoa, and Mendizábal 2008). Because of their uniqueness, our focus is on the two most exceptional steps that are taking place in the CAPV/EAE. These are aimed at preventing those youth who fail in school and drop out without any qualifications or basic training from remaining at-risk of being untrained and unemployed.

In these projects, the detection of good practices even if they were mitigating, provided us with the opportunity of participating in a scheme titled "Students at Risk of Educational Exclusion in Secondary Schools: Situational Programs and Best Practices." This project was coordinated from the University of Murcia by Professor Escudero Muñoz, and consisted of a team from that university, another from the University of Granada led by Professor Antonio Bolivar, and our own. During the academic years from 2006 to 2009 we carried out a study on the various socioeducational programs directed toward youth at risk of exclusion, using the methodology of case studies and biographical-narrative histories (Escudero and Bolivar 2008).

We are currently engaged in a project studying barriers and support in job training for young females who fail academically. In our earlier studies we found that academic failure in our school system has a very uneven impact in terms of gender. In fact, while 75 percent of the students failing basic studies are male, 91 percent of females are able to complete postcompulsory secondary education. However, of those young women who fail in school, a much lower percentage attends professional training centers. And when they do so, they select traditionally "feminized" professional profiles with worse job entry prospects. For all the reasons mentioned, in the current project we are focusing our attention in detecting different barriers to and support systems for the social and vocational world encountered by young women who fail in school. We have available to us the cooperation of students interested in sharing their life histories. The various steps taken to address diversity issues in the CAPV/EAE are found in table 2.1.

The Most Recent Empirical Study

Our most recent study is aimed at analyzing the two most excluding measures that have been designed for addressing diversity issues within the context of the CAPV/EAE: supplementary schooling programs and professional training programs. Since the implementation of the LOE, these professional training qualification programs are regulated by the educational administration and have specific curricular features that are mandated by law.[3]

---

3. See Martínez, Mendizabal, and Pérez-Sostoa (2009). The *Programas de Iniciación Profesional* [professional training programs] are regulated by Decree 72/2001, on April 24, establishing the essential elements of the educational steps involved in the Social Guarantee Programs (*Official Gazette of the Basque Country*, hereinafter BOPV, May 8, 2001); the *Programas Complementarios de Escolarización* [supplementary schooling programs] are regulated by the order of July 30, 1998 (BOPV, August 31, 1998), later modified by that of May 7, 2002 (BOPV, May 9, 2002), whereby educational activities are regulated for students in underprivileged social or cultural situations; chapter 5 sets forth its scheme for the supplementary schooling programs.

Table 2.1. Current programs to address diversity in the CAPV/EAE

Regular	Specific	Extraordinary
Schools's Curricular Project Plan intended to address diversity of the entire student body Classrooom scheduling adapted to group diversity Sequence of activities by levels Group activities Applying tasks to various situations Systematic inclusion of reinforcement and enrichment activities Individualized followup Optional: – Classroom tutorial – Individual tutorial – Educational group reinforcement. Groups with difficulties: – Break up group – Reduced faculty – Two instructors in one classroom – Workshops – Follow up by instructional team	Educational reinforcement Various strategies to address delays in crucial areas. The most common: – Outside the academic and classroom schedule, under an instructor's attention. – Individualized followup of students' work during set times outside of the regular academic schedule. – Individualized work plan/ personal contract between student and tutor or instructor. Diversity and Cooperation Program Aimed at improving the process of getting along in the classroom and overcoming inappropriate behaviors, learning to overcome conflict situations in a peaceful and civilized manner.	Students with special education needs: – Individual curricular adjustments. – Classrooms for learning tasks. – Expanding or reducing instructional time Staying an extra year. Curricular Diversification Program aimed at attaining basic goals and degrees: – Students between ages 16 and 18, with serious academic delay and a good attitude – Fields of knowledge in sociolinguistic and scientific-technological areas – Small and homogeneous group – Lasting 1 or 2 years Specific Educational Intervention Projects: – Students aged 12–13, with serious academic delay, underprivileged social situations and/or serious difficulties in adapting to the school setting – School project – Reduced number of teachers and group size – Reinforce tutorial action. – Lasting 2 to 4 academic years Intercultural program: – Foreign student inclusion – Welcoming program – Linguistic reinforcement classrooms Supplementary Schooling Program (developed in the study)
		Outside regular school Professional Training Qualification Programs (developed in the study)

Research Design

Our research consists of five phases. During the exploratory phase, a review was done of other studies and interviews with responsible parties and professionals from administration and educational inspection and support services in the area (the latter known collectively as Berritzegunes). This made it possible to detect the most important relevant parameters, and to design the instruments for compiling information.

During the second and third phases, we visited twenty-five vocational training centers. Also, we compiled and analyzed the information obtained from interviewing those in charge and studying the documentation. This made it possible to learn the track record of these centers and of the youth involved. The information collected subsequently through questionnaires submitted to students and faculty was triangulated in a discussion group that took place with representatives from all centers, on the following parameters: personal and academic track record of the students, assessment on the organizational and curricular aspects of the programs, need for faculty training, keys for success, and items for improvement.

The fourth phase relates to the work performed in the second project. It involved a narrative biographical study of twelve youths who volunteered to participate anonymously. They represented various track records and personal features in students successfully completing studies in these programs, after having failed in regular schools. Thus, we greatly valued their testimony.

The process has allowed us to study the range from mass statistics to personal experiences, compiling information on systems, practices, and vital impacts resulting from those relevant measures. Information about the sampling and participants in our study can be found in table 2.2.

Table 2.2. Sampling/participants

Number of schools, students, and teachers participating						
By ownership			Students			Teachers	
City hall	Entity	Subsidized Private	Supplementary program	Vocational program	Basic	Workshop
13	5	6	90	338	56	102

Results

The results of this comprehensive study are broken down into four parts relating to Professional Training Centers, student body, faculty, and overall pedagogical results.

Professional Training Centers

Professional training centers first appeared in the CAPV/EAE in 1985 through cooperation agreements between the Department of Education and various nonprofit agencies, to develop the first professional training programs.

Within the LOGSE framework, social guarantee programs are regulated as a compensatory and postcompulsory educational modality followed outside of regular schools to address the diversity of youth aged sixteen through twenty-one. There is agreement to reinforce basic training, professional orientation, and tutoring in the CAPV/EAE.

During the 2000–01 academic year, supplementary schooling programs were developed exclusively in the CAPV/EAE. This measure could be developed in regulated centers. However, having seen the serious difficulties in social and/or academic adaptation of the students this measure addresses, and its similarity to the professional training programs in modular design and workshops, since their first year of implementation these programs have also been developed in professional training centers.

Due to the LOE educational reform, professional training programs have again been modified in order to comply with the framework curricular design requirements of the current Professional Training Qualification Programs.

As one can imagine social, work, and educational changes over the more than three decades since the creation of the first centers and programs have had a major impact on the diversity of agencies, professionals, students, facilities, professional profiles, and practice centers that have shared this experience from academic year to year.

Nevertheless, a combination of certain variables detected (financial situation, type of ownership—public, private, subsidized, or subcontracted—and the socio-cultural context, together with educational priority) makes it possible to outline three profiles of centers, in terms of their greater or lesser concern for maintaining a balance between the need for integration into the labor force, the intent to limit the risk of marginal behaviors, or rejoining the academic world, earlier abandoned as a consequence of scholastic failure.

Student Body

Although diversity may be one of the most important features of the students arriving at these centers, certain common and different traits are seen in the youngest students who arrive for the supplementary schooling program and those who come to enroll in the professional training program.

Supplementary Program Students

Our study has developed this profile of supplementary program students. Most are fifteen years old, although each academic year more fourteen-year-old students join, and only rarely some aged thirteen. Most have serious behavioral problems and reject school: 20 percent have unstructured families, 80 percent some drug involvement, and 5 percent are in trouble with the law. Many have a long history of school failure, and may have had other measures available throughout schooling, but lack motivation for studying or working. Finally, we have recently noted a correlation with late entry into the system. Sometimes it relates to unusual legal status, students without families, and students with serious problems in terms of adaptability deficiencies.

Professional Training Program Students

Our study has developed this profile of professional training program students. Generally they are students who have successfully participated in a supplementary schooling program at the same center. Students who arrive from secondary schools are so far behind that they have not been selected from a Diversification Program. Many students, however, do come from a specific educational intervention project. This program takes place in regular schools with students from clearly disadvantaged social and family backgrounds. Finally, many are immigrant students with a vague legal status and covered by social services, interested in finding work and normalizing their situation.

Regarding their school track records before arriving at the professional training center, the data contained in their files and the information provided by the students themselves reveals a diverse body, although they do share common traits. First, they generally have a long history of academic failure; few students know exactly the last time they received passing grades in all subjects. Most feel responsible for their failure and attribute it their lack of effort, lack of interest in what had to be studied, absences, poor behavior, and so on. Howeve, there is a clear uncertainty in the criteria for advancement and for being assigned to the programs addressing diversity issues they have been part of. And finally, major dissonance exists between actual learning achievements and the results reflected by their grades.

Teachers

Initial training and career development of teachers is quite varied. The same is true of their social and professional status. Nevertheless, certain characteristics exist, more attitudinal and ethical, which appear to be shared by the most appreciated and successful teachers.

- Believing in students as individuals and in their capacity as apprentices.
- Educating without prejudices, starting from ground zero, conveying an image of capability, willingness, and possibility.
- Establishing a relationship based on respect, affection, and trust. Available as a contact or referral. By means of consistency, earning the right to demand accountability.
- Offering without discouragement new opportunities, exploring new ways, recognizing each and every small effort and achievement, seeking specific and custom solutions.
- Being aware of the impact in each student of his or her parameters: family, school, social, and labor market–related, and helping him or her to put together a plan for a dignified and attainable future.
- Teaching to walk by being a companion along the way. Starting with a first and simple step. Then one after the other. Getting up after falling. Correcting one's own mistakes. Seeking new ways and alternatives paths.
- Acknowledges "being in charge" of each vulnerable student, but without attempting to do it alone. Seeks assistance and balance from all community resources and individuals.

Pedagogical Model

What differentiates these centers from others, and what they have in common at the same time, in spite of their diversity, is the change in their way of *perceiving*, of *relating to*, and of *approaching* these young people, by no longer looking upon them as "failures." Starting from this changed outlook, the remaining features constituting their pedagogical model become even more significant.

The first feature of this model is a positive, wholesome image, with real prospects for the future of the students. Most of them share three basic opinions regarding their students: that in terms of possibilities, all are capable of developing the basic elements of learning that they need to be trained in; that for a proper diagnosis of students' needs and to structure the learning they are offered, they must be universally perceived as individuals and citizens, not just as a student of a module and/or course; and that as the young people they are, it is necessary to perceive them and they must perceive themselves as "having a present and a future."

Educational relationships must be created that are based on trust, respect, requirements, and rules of coexistence. The curricular and organizational conditions of the programs favor creating a climate of socio-emotional support in the classroom and at the center as a whole. Therefore, students' needs must be seen as the pivotal point of departure in the creation of the project curriculum. The framework curricular design is adapted to each context and student, starting with as much knowledge of each specific student as possible, as well as taking maximum advantage of four features of great didactic and educational potential in the programs: the possibility of integrating academic learning, technical capabilities and social abilities into projects related to professional profiles; new arenas of civic and practical learning as provided by workshops and practical training at company sites; stress must be given to how basic training and professional training are related, and how this training relates to entry into society and the labor market; and the overall organization of content in areas and fields of knowledge.

It is imperative that there be continuous follow up of progress to avoid stagnation, and possible setbacks in social, academic, and professional learning. Moreover, this should be accompanied by support in the transition to adult life required by the labor market. This is key element for purposes of establishing a link with the company where their practical training is taking place, prior to their potential hiring.

This model also calls for a transformation of the teaching role. Teachers should be seen as mediators, making available to students the tools necessary to perform activities. And as teachers, in the sense of leaders and role models the word conveys. This entails working as a team with the entire educational community, understood in the broadest sense. There should be coordinated intervention and good communication flowing between all interested individuals, and those vitally related to the students. Finally there must be recourse to all field resources and services. Each youth is perceived as a personal and specific project and as an opportunity to establish new liaisons with different resources in the field, which may be able to provide answers to his or her multiple needs.

Conclusion

We have here described a number of available resources that are available at the training centers and stemming from the Educational Administration of the CAPV/EAE. These resources are making it possible for a percentage of students at risk of dropping out, failing, or being expelled to find new opportunities and new venues for learning and socializing, thereby avoiding the risk of social exclusion (Irakas Sistema Ebaluatu eta Ikertzeko Erakundea /Instituto Vasco de Evaluación e Investigación Educativa 2007, 2008, 2009).

The steps for addressing diversity issues also cover a broad spectrum of vulnerability between the more serious possibility of exclusion and the more satisfactory possibility of inclusion. However, they offer only marginal answers that do not guarantee to an important segment of students the achievement of essential elements of learning.

Paradoxically, the development of all the steps for addressing diversity issues, and particularly in the case of the most drastic steps, is often having as an undesired outcome the fact that regular schools, classrooms, and teachers deem it unnecessary to review the rationale of exclusion and thus perpetuate the established rigid and elitist organization of academia. In effect, the system is essentially self-perpetuating (Escudero 2009).

The positive and negative aspects of the adopted steps resemble similar programs that are underway in other autonomous communities of the Spanish state (Feito, García, and Casal 2006; Marhuenda 2006; Sánchez 2004; Vélaz de Medrano 2005) and further afield (Alliance for Excellent Education 2008; Cole 2008; Hammond et al. 2007; Jonson and Rudolph 2001; Munn 2007).

In view of the challenge represented by the development of the LOE reform and the goals proposed in the European context regarding failure reduction and increase in the percentage of the population with secondary education, we believe in the need to publicize, acknowledge, and transfer the keys to the good practices that have been taking place in the CAPV/EAE in connection with the measures for addressing diversity issues. The results obtained in the CAPV/EAE in compulsory education—when compared with the Spanish state in general—are due in large part to those measures.

Nevertheless, faced with the risk of dual instructional standards, which is starting to become evident between the schools, classrooms, programs, and students deemed "regular" and those involved in more specific and exceptional measures, we see the need to continue short-term and medium-term research on improving those measures and incorporating their good practices into regular instruction. There is also the need to ask the administrators and the educational community—and Basque society in general—to supervise and make sure that the excuse of "addressing diversity issues" is not generating new forms of labeling and segregating the most vulnerable students.

References

Alliance for Excellent Education. 2008. *From No Child Left Behind to Every Child a Graduate.* Washington, DC: Alliance for Excellent Education.

Bennet, Albert et al. 2004. *All Students Reaching the Top: Strategies for Closing Academia Achievement Gaps.* New York: North Central Regional Educational Laboratory. Learning Point.

Bolívar, Antonio, and Gijón, José. 2008. "Historias de vida que deshacen profecías de fracaso." *Cuadernos de Pedagogía* 382: 56–59.

Castel, Robert. 2004. "Encuadre de la exclusión." In *La exclusión: Bordeando sus fronteras. Definiciones y matices*, coord. Saül Karsz. Barcelona: Gedisa.

Cole, Robert, ed. 2008. *Educating Everybody's Children: Diverse Strategies for Diverse Learners.* 2nd edition. Texas: Association for Supervision and Curriculum Development.

Departamento de Educación, Universidades e Investigación. 1982. *Plan de Educación Especial para el País Vasco.* Vitoria-Gasteiz: Servicio Central de Publicaciones del Gobierno Vasco.

Escudero, Juan Manuel. 2005. "Fracaso Escolar, Exclusión Educativa: ¿De qué se excluye y cómo?" *Profesorado: Revista de currículum y formación del profesorado* 9, no 1: 1–24.

———. 2009. "Buenas prácticas y programas extraordinarios de atención al alumnado en riesgo de exclusión educativa." *Profesorado: Revista de currículum y formación del profesorado* 13, no 3: 107–41.

Escudero, Juan Manuel, and Antonio Bolívar. 2008. "Respuestas organizativas y pedagógicas ante el riesgo de exclusión educativa." In *Organizaciones educativas al servicio de la sociedad*, ed. Joaquin Gairín and Serafín Antúnez. Barcelona: Wolters Kluwer Educación.

Escudero, Juan Manuel, Mª Teresa González, and Begoña Martínez. 2009. "El fracaso escolar como exclusión educativa: Comprensión, políticas y prácticas." *Revista Iberoamericana de Educación* 50, no 2: 41–64.

Feito, Rafael, Maribel García, and Joaquín Casal. 2006. "De los Programas de Garantía Social a los Programas de Cualificación Profesional Inicial. Sobre perfiles y dispositivos locales." *Revista de Educación* 341, no 1: 81–98.

Galarreta, Javier, Begoña Martínez, José Ramón Orcasitas, and Virginia Pérez-Sostoa. 1999. *La formación de profesionales de apoyo al sistema educativo. Perfiles y servicios.* Donostia: Erein.

———. 2000. "Los programas de diversificación curricular, una propuesta de atención a la diversidad en la ESO." In Various Authors, *Hacia el tercer milenio. Cambio educativo y educación para el cambio.* Madrid: Sociedad Española de Pedagogía.

Galarreta, Javier, Begoña Martínez, Amaia Mendizabal, José Ramón Orcasitas, and Virginia Pérez-Sostoa. 2003. "La respuesta a la diversidad en la eso de la CAV. ¿Un camino hacia la inclusión?" In *Educación y diversidades. Formación, Acción, Investigación,* coord. Carmen Buisán. Barcelona: Universidad de Barcelona.

Galarreta, Javier, Begoña Martínez, Amaia Mendizabal, José Ramón Orcasitas, and Virginia Pérez-Sostoa. 2006. "Los Proyectos de Intervención Específica en la CAV. ¿Una oportunidad para evitar la exclusión del alumnado en la ESO?" In *Atención a la Diversidad. Una responsabilidad compartida,* ed. Jerónima Ipland et al. Huelva: Universidad de Huelva.

Hammond, Cynthia et al. 2007. *Dropout Risk Factors and Exemplary Programs: A Technical Report.* Clemson, SC: National Dropout Prevention Center/Network.

Instituto Vasco de Evaluación e Investigación Educativa (ISEI/IVEI). 2007. *Abandono Escolar en 3º y 4º de la ESO.* Bilbao: Departamento de Educación, Universidades e Investigación, Gobierno Vasco.

———. 2008. *Finalización de la Secundaria Obligatoria.* Bilbao: Departamento de Educación, Universidades e Investigación, Gobierno Vasco.

———. 2009. *Efecto de las repeticiones de curso en el proceso de enseñanza-aprendizaje del alumnado.* Bilbao: Departamento de Educación, Universidades e Investigación, Gobierno Vasco.

Jonson, Debra, and Rudolph, Angela. 2001. "Performance Pentagon: Five Strategies to Help All Students Make the Grade." *NASSP Bulletin* 85, no 12: 40–55.

——. 2006. *Critical Issue: Beyond Social Promotion and Retention: Five Strategies to Help Students Succeed.* Naperville, IL: North Central Regional Educational. Learning Point Associates. At www.ncrel.org/sdrs/areas/issues/students/atrisk/at800.htm.

Luengo, Julián, comp. 2007. *Paradigmas de gobernación y de exclusión social en la educación. Fundamentos para el análisis de la discriminación escolar contemporánea.* Barcelona-México: Pomares.

Marhuenda, Fernando. 2006. "La formación para el empleo de jóvenes sin graduado: educación, capacitación y socialización para la integración social." *Revista de Educación* 341, no 1: 15–34.

Martínez, Begoña. 2001. "Hacia un modelo de apoyo al centro para mejorar el tratamiento de la diversidad." In *Atención Educativa a la Diversidad en el nuevo milenio*, coord. Juan José Bueno, Teresa Núñez, and Ana Iglesias. A Coruña: Universidade da Coruña.

——. 2002. "La educación en la diversidad en los albores del siglo XXI." In *Educación, diversidad y calidad de vida*, edited by Dolores Forteza and Mª Rosa Rosselló. Palma de Mallorca: Universitat de les Illes Balears.

——. 2004. "Senderos que bordean la inclusión educativa en la ESO." In *Cambiar con la sociedad, cambiar la sociedad. Actas del 8º Congreso Interuniversitario de Organización*, edited by Julián López et al. Sevilla: Universidad de Sevilla.

——. 2005. "Las medidas de respuesta a la diversidad: posibilidades y límites para la inclusión escolar y social." *Profesorado. Revista de currículum y formación del profesorado* 9, no 1: 1–31.

——. 2008a. "Puentes entre el fracaso escolar y un nuevo escenario sociolaboral." *Cuadernos de Pedagogía* 382: 67–69.

——. 2008b. "Respuestas de los Centros de Iniciación Profesional para evitar la exclusión sociolaboral de jóvenes vulnerables." In *Organizaciones educativas al servicio de la sociedad*, edited by Joaquín Gairín and Serafín Antúnez. Barcelona: Wolters Kluwer Educación.

Martínez, Begoña, Virginia Pérez-Sostoa, and Amaia Mendizabal. 2008. "Exclusión y Educación para la ciudadanía. Valoración de una experiencia realizada con jóvenes que fracasan en la escuela." In Various Authors, *Actas del XIX Congreso Nacional y III Iberoamericano de*

Pedagogía: Educación, ciudadanía y convivencia. Zaragoza: Sociedad Española de Pedagogía & Universidad de Zaragoza.

Martínez, Begoña, Amaia Mendizabal, and Virginia Pérez-Sostoa. 2009. "Una Oportunidad para que los jóvenes que fracasan en la escuela puedan salir de la zona de riesgo de exclusión. La experiencia de los Centros de Iniciación Profesional en la Comunidad Autónoma Vasca." *Profesorado. Revista de currículum y formación del* profesorado 13, no 3: 239–71.

Munn, Geoffrey. 2007. "A Sense of Wonder: Pedagogies to Engage Students Who Live in Poverty." *International Journal of Inclusive Education* 11, no 3: 301–15.

Orcasitas, José Ramón. 2005. "20 años de integración escolar en el País Vasco: haciendo historia. Construyendo un Sistema Educativo de calidad para todos." In Various Authors, *La respuesta a las necesidades educativas especiales en una Escuela Vasca inclusiva.* Actas del Congreso"Guztientzako Eskola," Donostia-San Sebastián, October 29–31, 2003. Vitoria-Gasteiz: Servicio Central de Publicaciones del Gobierno Vasco.

Parrilla, Ángeles, Carmen Gallego, and Anabel Moriña. 2009. "El complicado tránsito a la vida activa de jóvenes en riesgo de exclusión: Una perspectiva biográfica." *Revista de Educación* 351, no 1: 211–233.

Pérez-Sostoa, Virginia, and Begoña Martínez. "El perfil del profesorado de apoyo. Un modelo formativo." In Various Authors, *XIII Jornadas de Universitat y Educación Especial.* Barcelona: Universidad de Barcelona.

Popkewitz, Thomas, and Sverker Lindblad. 2007. "Gobernación educativa e inclusión y exclusión social: dificultades conceptuales y problemáticas en la política y en la investigación." In *Paradigmas de gobernación y de exclusión social en la educación. Fundamentos para el análisis de la discriminación escolar contemporánea,* ed. Julián Luengo. Barcelona-México: Pomares.

Sánchez, Antonio, coord. 2004. *De los Programas de Garantía Social a los Programas de iniciación Profesional. Pensamiento del profesorado y del alumnado.* Barcelona: Alertes.

Sellman, Edgard. 2009. "Lessons Learned: Student Voice at a School for Pupils Experiencing Social, Emotional and Behavioural Difficulties." *Emotional and Behavioral Difficulties* 14, no 1: 33–48.

Sen, Amartya, and Bernardo Kliksberg. 2008. *Primero la gente. Una mirada desde la ética del desarrollo a los principales problemas del mundo globalizado.* Barcelona: Deusto.

Subirats, Joan, ed. 2004. *Pobreza y exclusión social. Un análisis de la realidad española y europea.* Barcelona: Fundación La Caixa.

Susinos, Teresa. 2009. "Escuchar para compartir. Reconociendo la autoridad del alumnado en el proyecto de una escuela inclusiva." *Revista de Educación* 349: 119–36.

Tezanos, José Félix. 2001. *La sociedad dividida. Estructuras de clase y desigualdades en las sociedades tecnológicas.* Madrid: Biblioteca Nueva.

Vélaz de Medrano, Consuelo. 2005. "Cómo prevenir el rechazo y la exclusión social." *Cuadernos de Pedagogía* 348, no 7: 58–61.

3

Improving Social Interaction: Experimentally Validated Proposals for Psycho-educational Intervention

MAITE GARAIGORDOBIL and JONE ALIRI

Considering certain current local and global social situations (school violence, gender violence, racism, endless armed conflicts), educating for peace and nonviolence has become a primary educational goal, with the school as its privileged setting. In recent years there has been a significant change in the notion of education. Throughout history, the school has been considered an institution focused on intellectual development and academic achievement; however, there is increasingly an attempt to supersede this concept of the school as nothing more than an agent for transmitting knowledge, with efforts toward broadening educational processes to include education on values and attitudes for peaceful coexistence, in order to produce supportive, egalitarian, tolerant, and peaceful individuals.

From this vantage point, during the past twenty years as a group of professionals in psychology and education in the Comunidad Autónoma del País Vasco/Euskal Autonomia Erkidegoa (CAPV/EAE, Autonomous Community of the Basque Country), we have designed, applied, and assessed four programs of intervention that have been experimentally validated through four studies. The programs are aimed at promoting prosocial behavior, emotional development, and education on respecting human rights. Specifically, these programs of intervention stimulate the development of social-emotional factors related to respecting human rights, such as communication, relationships involving help and confidence, cooperation skills, empathy, emotional expression, respecting differences, and strategies for conflict resolution. This chapter examines an intervention area of interest in the development of ethical-moral values, and looks at the effects of cooperative play and group dynamics on human development.

The four JUEGO programs, which constitute a psycho-educational intervention area of interest, are structured with cooperative games and are aimed at enhancing social interaction and promoting social-emotional development and creativity in children. The programs have been implemented and experimentally validated in ten schools in the CAPV/ EAE. Their design and application began in 1989, and their implementation at various educational levels in numerous schools continues at the present time. Research studies have taken place with a sampling of 504 children, ages four through twelve. The evaluative results have shown a very positive effect on social and personal development factors, relating to values education, social interaction, and violence prevention. The evaluation of the JUEGO Program, ages six through eight, received the Special Doctorate Award from the Universidad del País Vasco/Euskal Herriko Unibertsitatea (UPV/EHU, University of the Basque Country), and the programs for ages eight through ten and ten through twelve received the First National Prize for Educational Research, 1994 and 2003, respectively, from the Spanish Ministry of Education and Science.

The Theoretical Basis

This study is theoretically based on the findings arising from two major research areas: child-play and prosocial behavior. Studies have confirmed that children's play, that quintessential childhood activity, is vital for human development, since it provides an important contribution to the psychomotor, intellectual, social, and affective-emotional development. Research studies on the contribution of play to child development have confirmed that play is an important engine in human development. This is because it has an important role in both social development, by empowering socialization, communication, and cooperation with peers (Ballou 2001; Carlson 1999; Cheah, Nelson, and Rubin 2001; Smith 2005); and affective-emotional development, by allowing emotional control and expression, favoring psychological balance, and improved self-concept (Gagnon and Tagle 2004; Moore and Russ 2008). Empirical evidence highlights that playing allows children to develop their thinking, satisfy their needs, explore and discover, learn the joy of creating, generate experiences, express and control emotions, broaden their horizons, and learn to cooperate. Therefore, nurturing cooperative, constructive, symbolic, and positive leisure activities in school settings is synonymous with empowering child development. In addition, research has shown that cooperative games requiring teamwork and mutual respect among group members reduce the level of rejection among classroom peers (Mikami, Boucher, and Humphreys 2005). Comparison studies between the effects of cooperative play programs and competitive play programs confirm the benefits of cooperation in the positive processes of socialization. Cooperative play programs resulted in a greater number of positive social behaviors (Finlinson, Austin, and Pfister 2000), fewer aggressive behaviors (Bay-Hinitz and Wilson 2005), and a higher level of negotiation strategies and sharing behaviors among group members (Zan and Hildebrandt 2003).

The second theoretical basis for our intervention programs concerns the results from research on prosocial behavior. These cooperative play proposals define prosocial behavior as all positive social behavior with or without altruistic motivation (behaviors such as giving, helping, cooperating, sharing, and comforting). Likewise, a cooperative situation is understood as one in which the goals of participating individuals are related in such a way that each can achieve his or her goal if and only if the others are able to achieve theirs; whereas a competitive situation would be one in which an individual's goals are achieved if and only if other individuals are not able to achieve theirs. The systematic study on the research, providing data in reference to variables that influence the development of prosocial behavior, confirms that the development of prosocial behavior is a complex matter since it depends on many factors. Prosocial behavior depends on multiple interrelated factors associated with culture, family setting, school environment, as well as others related to personal development (age, moral and cognitive development, ability to have a point of view, empathy). Nevertheless, and although prosocial behavior is mediated or determined by numerous situational and personality factors, the conclusions drawn from the studies that assess the effects of the prosocial behavior training programs confirm the effectiveness of interventions aimed at encouraging this type of behavior (Beilinson 2003; Carlson 1999; Dyson 2001; Mikami, Boucher, and Humphreys 2005; Miller et al. 2003; Roseth, Johnson, and Johnson 2008). Research on prosocial behavior has confirmed the important benefits of cooperative experiences on different elements of social and personal development, such as communication, conflict resolution, interpersonal relationships, satisfying affective needs, and academic performance. Specifically, the studies that have analyzed the effects of cooperating versus competing in educational settings have shown a positive effect on social development factors, since cooperative interaction encourages group cohesion; helps reduce intergroup conflicts; promotes prosocial behaviors within the group; reduces negative social behaviors; increases acceptance by group members; tolerance toward ethnically different people and toward individuals with physical and intellectual disabilities; improves classroom atmosphere and interpersonal relationships; and increases social abilities, problem-solving skills, and moral development in general. This is also true in terms of emotional development factors, since cooperative interaction fosters empathy, emotional decentralization, and improves self-esteem.

Cooperative Game Program Descriptions

I will now examine in detail the objectives of these cooperative game plans, the structural characteristics of the games, how they are shaped via different types of games, and the procedure employed to apply these experiences to any age group.

Game Programs Goals

The activities that constitute these cooperative and creative game programs have two general primary goals. They try to facilitate the comprehensive development of children who do not have difficulties in their growth, with special emphasis on various social-emotional aspects and the development of creativity. And they serve a therapeutic function, because these game-playing experiences are aimed at socially integrating children who have difficulties in interacting with their peers and/or difficulties in other aspects of their development. On a more concrete level, the programs have various specific goals that are outlined in table 3.1.

Table 3.1. Game program goals

Goals
Facilitate the development of socialization by encouraging: <ul><li>Children to get to know one another, increase friendly, positive, constructive, multidirectional interaction with group peers, and group participation</li><li>Friendly intra-group relationships</li><li>Verbal and nonverbal communication skills: to make a statement, to actively listen, to dialogue, to negotiate, to make decisions by consensus</li><li>An increase in social behaviors that facilitate socialization (leadership behavior, cheerfulness, being helpful, respect and self-control, assertive behavior), as well as a decrease in behavior that disrupts socialization (aggressive behavior, passive behavior, anxiety-shyness, apathy-withdrawal)</li><li>Prosocial behavior: relationships involving helpfulness and the ability to cooperate (giving and receiving help in order to contribute to common goals)</li><li>Moral development: accepting social rules related to the instructions for the games (taking turns, cooperative structure, roles) and with the rules coming from the group for purposes of carrying out the games</li></ul>
Fostering emotional development by encouraging: <ul><li>Identification of a variety of emotions</li><li>Expression of emotions through dramatization, activities with music-movement, drawing, and painting</li><li>Understanding of the different causes or situations that generate positive and negative emotions</li><li>Confronting or resolving negative emotions</li><li>Development of empathy when faced with emotional conditions in other human beings</li><li>Improvement of self-image</li></ul>
Nurture the development of intellectual factors, such as: <ul><li>Verbal, graphic, constructive, and social creativity, and drama</li><li>Attention, concentration</li><li>Memory</li><li>Symbolization skills</li></ul>

Features of Cooperation Games

Altogether, the games contained in the programs encourage communication, cohesion, confidence, and the development of creativity, and underlying them is the idea of accepting one another, cooperating, sharing, playing, and inventing together. The games selected to configure this program share five structural characteristics: (1) Participation, because in these games all group members participate, no one is ever eliminated, no one ever loses; the idea is to attain group goals, and for this to happen each participant has an essential role in the game. (2) Communication and friendly interaction, because all games in the program generate processes of communication within the group, which imply listening, dialoguing, making decisions, and negotiating. The games in this program encourage friendly multidirectional interaction among group members, the expression of positive feelings in relation to others, in order to gradually facilitate processes of cooperation. (3) Cooperation, since many of the games in the program promote relation dynamics that leads the players to help one another in order to contribute to a common end, a group goal. In these games, players' objectives are closely interrelated, so that each player can only reach his or her objectives if the others reach theirs. In cooperative games, each player contributes; the player's role is rich with meaning and is essential for the game to succeed. (4) Fiction and creation, because the games in the program are played along the lines of "as if" they were reality—as if we were butterflies, robots, blind people—as well as combining stimuli in order to create something new. (5) Fun, because through these games we are trying to generate fun for group members, for them to enjoy a positive, constructive interaction with their group peers. Cooperative games eliminate the fear of making a mistake and the anxiety related to failure. By playing cooperatively, participants learn to share and to help one another, to relate to others, to consider the feelings of others, and to contribute to common ends. These games promote a group feeling, but by acknowledging each individual within the group, they enable equality in relationships among players, facilitating cordial, friendly, and constructive relationships with empathy. These game programs have been developed with the aim of raising children's awareness of others, showing them through action the benefits of cooperation and nonaggression when interacting with peers.

Game Categories in the Programs

The four programs are structured within a set of activities, between 80 and 140 games, which encourage communication, prosocial behavior, and creativity. Program activities are divided into two major types of games: communication and prosocial behavior games, and cooperative games of creativity.

The module on *communication and pro-social behavior* games contains three types of games: communication-group cohesion games, help-confidence games, and cooperation games. Activities included within the category of *communication and group cohesion games* are intended to elicit communication within the group and a feeling of belonging to the group. These activities facilitate careful listening to others, paying active attention not only for purposes of understanding, but also being open to the needs and feelings of others. Games that involve forms of communication, be it verbal or nonverbal, account for innumerable experiences in terms of encouraging interpersonal relationships and strengthening the group, facilitating new possibilities in communication and greater openness in relationships, bringing them closer.

Within the category of *help and confidence games,* there are games generating relational situations where group members provide mutual help, because the game activity dynamics sets forth this type of action in order for the game to be able to continue. These games are intended to bolster in children the skill of perceiving others' needs and responding positively to those needs, thus improving supportive relationships among group members, as well as their own self-image. In addition, this category includes game activities that bolster self-confidence and encourage trusting others, because from this standpoint nurturing trust in the group is a requirement in order to generate the helpful attitudes necessary that can subsequently lead to group cooperation processes.

Cooperation games include those that encourage relational situations where group members help each other in order to contribute to a common end. These are games where cooperation between players is an essential element for purposes of performing the activity; without this element the game's goal is impossible to reach. These games based on the idea of participation, acceptance, and cooperation by having fun, imply one additional step in the process of overcoming competitive relationships, developing in the individual the skills of cooperating and sharing.

Within the module on *cooperative games of creativity,* the category of *verbal creativity games* contains activities that encourage verbal communication and active listening habits, language development, use of words in reasoning skills, and the ability to create by means of words, thus nurturing several indicators of verbal creativity. The category of *drama creativity games* contains game activities that encourage cooperative interaction, while creating an avenue for comprehensive self-expression of the child's personality, through drama fiction. In these games, emotions find a channel of expression and freedom, in addition to serving as a way of communicating with others. The purpose of these games is not to provide a good performance, but to make it possible for children to go from a passive listening phase to a more active one involving delivery and creation. *Graphic-figurative creativity games,* in addition to promoting verbal communication and active listening habits, encourage cooperation and creativity in tasks related to drawing and painting. In the category of *plastic-constructive creativity games,* included activities help improve analytical skills, and cooperation in cognitive tasks, which involves combining stimuli in order to construct new objects, new products.

Procedure for Applying the Programs with a Group

Applying the game programs with a group involves three phases: the *pre-test assessment phase* takes place during the first weeks of the academic year. This phase includes an assessment prior to the intervention, aimed at exploring different variables in child development. The hypothesis is that the program is going to have a positive effect on those variables (intra-group communication, prosocial behavior, negative social behaviors for socializing, self-concept, creativity). Thereafter, the *phase for applying game program* consists of implementing one weekly game session, variable in length, from 75 minutes (program for ages four to six), to 90 minutes (programs for ages six to eight and eight to ten), and 120 minutes (program for ages ten to twelve), throughout the entire academic year. Game sessions involve a sequence of two or three cooperative activities, followed by discussions. Each session consists of three phases: the opening phase of the session, the game sequence development phase, and the closure phase. The intervention took place in the same physical space, a large barrier-free classroom, on the same day of the week and at the same time of the day. The game experience is directed by an adult, usually the group's regular teacher, with the help of an observer. Finally, in *the post-test assessment phase,* which takes place during the last weeks of the school year, the same instruments as in the pretest phase are administered, with the goal of evaluating any change in the development factors measured.

Program Assessment Instruments

In order to evaluate the effects of the programs, before and after the intervention and at each age level several assessment instruments were administered, for the purpose of measuring the dependent variables that were the basis for the hypothesis that the program was going to have an effect (see table 3.2a-d). The references to assessment instruments can be checked in the manuals for the programs.

Table 3.2a. Program variables and assessment instruments, ages four to six

	Variables assessed	Assessment instruments
Factors in social and affective-emotional development	Cognitive strategies for prosocial resolution of interpersonal problems	Test for interpersonal problem resolution
	Altruism: sharing with peers and with adults	Altruism assessment
	Emotional stability	Human figure drawing test
	Self-concept	Self-concept scale
	Behaviors: adaptability, aggressiveness, anxiety, atypicality, depression, hyperactivity, social skills, attention problems, somatization, withdrawal	System for Behavior Assessment in Children and Adolescents (teachers and parents)
Intellectual and maturity development factors	Intelligence: verbal, nonverbal, total	Brief test for intelligence
	Neuropsychological maturity factors	Questionnaire for neuropsychological maturity in children
	Development factors	Observational scale for development (parents)
Creativity	Creative personality behaviors and traits	Scale for creative personality behaviors and traits (parents and teachers)
	Verbal creativity, graphic-figurative creativity	Test on creative thinking: Verbal and graphic battery
	Creative thinking	Test on creative thought by analyzing an image

Table 3.2b. Ages six to eight

	Variables assessed	Assessment instruments
Factors in social and affective-emotional development	Positive and negative social behaviors for socialization	Socialization battery (teachers)
	Image of group peers	Sociometric questionnaire (group peers)
	Cognitive strategies for social interaction: direct, indirect, aggressive	Questionnaire on cognitive strategies for social interaction
	Group cooperation skill	Assess group cooperation: The squares game
	Self-concept	Self-concept scale
	Emotional stability	Human figure drawing test
Intelligence and creativity factors	Creative personality behaviors and traits	Scale for creative personality behaviors and traits (parents and teachers)
	Maturity aptitudes for academic learning	Battery of aptitudes for academic learning
	Body diagram	Test for recognizing body diagram

3.2c. Ages eight to ten

	Variables assessed	Assessment instruments
Factors in social and affective-emotional development	Non-altruistic behavior	Experimental technique for assessing altruistic behavior: The prisoner's dilemma
	Social behavior: assertive, passive, aggressive	Self-report on social behavior: Assertive behavior scale in children
	Social behavior: help	Socialization battery. Social awareness scale (teachers)
	Intra-group communication: positive-negative messages	Intra-group communication assessment: The silhouette game (group peers)
	Self-concept: body, intellectual, social, emotional	Adjective Check List for self-concept assessment
Creativity	Verbal creativity	Guilford battery
	Graphic creativity	Guilford battery; Abreaction Test for assessing creativity

3.2d. Ages ten to twelve

	Variables assessed	Assessment instruments
Factors in social and affective-emotional development	Social behaviors: caring for others, leadership, self-control, withdrawal, anxiety.	Socialization battery (self-assessment)
	Antisocial behavior	Questionnaire on antisocial-delinquent behaviors
	Prosocial behavior	Questionnaire on prosocial behavior (teachers and parents)
	Prosocial and creative peers	Sociometric Questionnaire: prosocial and creative peer (group peers)
	Social behavior: assertive, aggressive, passive	Assertive behavior scale in children
	Cognitive strategies for resolving social situations	Questionnaire on cognitive strategies for solving social situations
	Self-concept	Adjective Check List for overall and creative self-concept assessment
	Emotional stability	Human figure drawing test
Intelligence and creativity factors	Intelligence: verbal, nonverbal, total.	Brief test for intelligence
	Creative personality behaviors and traits	Creative personality scale (self-assessment, parents and teachers)
	Verbal associative thinking	Word association test
	Verbal creativity, graphic creativity	Torrance's test of creative thinking
	Graphic creativity	Freely create a painting. Inter-judges assessment of creative product.

Experimental Studies for Evaluating the Programs

The purpose of the experimental studies carried out with the four programs has been to evaluate their effects on different variables of social development, affective-emotional development, intelligence, and child creativity. The four studies validating these experiences have used an experimental multi-group design with repeated pretest and posttest measurements of specific control groups. The procedure followed in the studies consists of three phases. At the beginning of the academic year, a pretest assessment was performed by giving experimental and control subjects different evaluation tests in order to measure different variables, over which the program was supposedly going to have an effect (see table 3.2a-d). Subsequently, the intervention program was implemented for each age level with the experimental groups. The application consisted of administering one cooperative weekly game session lasting 75–90–120 minutes (depending on age), during the entire academic year. Finally, at the end of the school year a posttest assessment was made again, applying to the entire sample the same assessment instruments as in the pretest phase.

Implementation of the programs was carried out by teachers of the groups randomly selected from public and private schools in the CAPV/ EAE. The groups were first formed, while the application of assessment instruments was performed at the schools by psychologists who cooperated in the development of subsequent projects. The procedure followed in the studies involved compliance with ethical provisions regarding human experimentation included in the Declaration of Helsinki.

In order to assess change in the variables under study, descriptive analyses were performed (mean and standard deviations of each variable in experimental and control subjects, in the pretest phase, the posttest phase, and the posttest-pretest difference) and inferential analyses (univariate and multivariate analyses of variance: ANOVAs, ANCOVAs, MANOVAs, and MANCOVAs). The results obtained in the experimental assessment of the four JUEGO Programs have confirmed the positive effects these types of cooperative experiences have on various social, emotional, and intellectual elements of child development. The results obtained in the studies have validated this line of psycho-educational intervention, based on cooperative games for personality development in children ages four through twelve.

The program focused on boys and girls in childhood education (Garaigordobil 2007) was experimentally validated through a study of eighty-six subjects, ages five to six, distributed in five groups. Of the eighty-six children in the sample, fifty-three were exposed to the game program (three groups) and thirty-three served as control (two groups). The intervention consisted of one weekly cooperative game session, seventy-five minutes in length, during the entire academic year. The evaluation of the program confirmed that this playing experience had significantly triggered an improvement in psychomotor, intellectual, social, and affective-emotional development factors. From the social and emotional development standpoint, the program resulted in a significant increase in altruistic pro-social behavior with group peers, the capability of prosocial resolution of interpersonal problems, awareness of and compliance with social standards pointed out by adults, and affective maturity or the capability of providing affective responses in alignment with the developmental (trend) level. From the cognitive and psychomotor development standpoint, the program furthered an increase in: verbal intelligence (Verbal

IQ), neuropsychological maturity factors such as verbal fluency, verbal creativity (fluency, flexibility, originality), graphic-figurative creativity (abreaction, processing, fluency, originality), behaviors and traits typical of creative personalities, and creative thinking associated with the analysis of an image (ability to perceive unusual or rare details, fluency and originality in identifying problems and seeking solutions to these problems).

Research on the program for children ages six through eight (Garaigordobil 2005a) took place with 178 subjects distributed in eight groups; six of these groups (125 subjects) were randomly assigned experimental status, while two groups (53 subjects) served as control subjects. The intervention consisted of implementing one weekly game session, ninety minutes in length. Variance analyses performed with the data obtained in the assessments confirmed a positive impact of the game program on children's development. From the social development standpoint, the program facilitated: an increase in positive social behaviors (leadership, cheerfulness, social awareness, respect-self control), and a reduction in negative social behaviors (aggressiveness-stubbornness, apathy-withdrawal, anxiety-shyness) in social interactions with peers, as well as an improvement in overall social adaptation in children within the school setting; an increase in group cooperation skills and of intra-group communications (interactions of acceptance); and a lesser use of aggressive cognitive strategies as a technique for resolving social conflicts. From the affective-emotional standpoint the program fostered and improvement in: self-concept and emotional stability. At the psychomotor and cognitive development level, the program facilitated: a superior evolution of the body diagram and of various maturity aptitudes for academic learning (verbal comprehension, numerical aptitude, perceptive aptitude).

The program study for children ages eight through ten (Garaigordobil 2003) took place with 154 subjects divided into five groups. Of these, four groups were experimental (126 subjects) and one served as control group (28 subjects). The intervention consisted of applying one weekly game session, ninety minutes in length. The results of variance analyses, performed with the data obtained in the assessments, highlighted a positive impact of the program, by having fostered in terms of social development: an increase in altruistic prosocial behavior, a reduction in nonassertive (passive-aggressive) social behaviors in the interaction with peers, an increase in positive messages in intra-group communications, and a reduction in negative messages. As far as affective-emotional development was concerned, the program facilitated an improvement in: all-round self-concept, particularly in reference to affective and social self-concept. At the cognitive development level, a significant increase was also verified: in verbal creativity (fluency, flexibility, originality), and in graphic-figurative creativity (fluency, flexibility, originality, connectedness, abreaction, fantasy). The results obtained validated the program (Garaigordobil 1994).

The experimental validation of the game program for children ages ten to twelve (Garaigordobil 2004) was performed with eighty-six subjects distributed in four groups; of these, two groups (fifty-four subjects) served as experimental, and two groups (thirty-two subjects) served as control during that academic year. The intervention consisted of implementing one weekly game session, two hours long. The results of variance analyses highlighted a positive impact of the program by having facilitated from the social development standpoint an increase in: social behaviors that show respect toward socialization rules and self-control of impulses, social behaviors of leadership related to the spirit of service and popularity, assertive behaviors in interaction with peers, prosocial behaviors, the perception of group peers seen as more prosocial and creative, and cognitive strategies of assertive social interaction. A reduction was also verified in aggressive behaviors when interacting with peers and antisocial behaviors. From the affective-emotional development standpoint, the program facilitated an increase in emotional stability and an improvement in self-concept. In terms of cognitive development, a positive impact of the program was confirmed in verbal intelligence (verbal IQ), verbal creativity (originality), graphic-figurative creativity (abreaction, originality, and processing), and behaviors and traits typical of creative personalities (Garaigordobil 2005b).

The results obtained in evaluating the four programs have been published in numerous national and international journals of educational and psychological research, which can be consulted and downloaded from the web at www.sc.ehu.es/garaigordobil.

Findings

The results obtained from evaluating these programs corroborate other studies that have confirmed the positive effects of cooperative play on various social-emotional development factors. The work undertaken since 1989 has provided empirical evidence of the positive contribution of games, and has made it possible to systematize intervention tools for human development in these developmental stages, which consist of cooperative play activities and debates regarding personal beliefs and the conflicts that arise from interpersonal relationships. The four studies have confirmed that these programs enhance social-emotional development, foster social interaction, and play a role in the prevention of violence, which is especially valuable in the education of children in the Basque Country.

In addition, the study has made it possible to confirm that games are powerful instruments for communicating and socializing. Games can be a means for educating on values, since all group play activities that children engage in throughout childhood promote the gradual development of the child's social "self." Studies that have researched the effects of cooperative play have confirmed that these games encourage communication, promote positive messages among group members, increase prosocial behaviors (helping, cooperating, sharing, comforting), reduce negative social behaviors (aggressiveness-stubbornness, apathy-withdrawal, anxiety-shyness), facilitate participation and group cohesion improving the social atmosphere in the classroom, and elevate self-concept and the concept of others.

Nevertheless, for a game to enhance moral development, it needs to include specific social interactions. The games facilitating the development of moral-ethical values and prosocial behavior are those that encourage communication, cohesion, and confidence among group members, based on the idea of being accepted, cooperating, and sharing. Currently the JUEGO Programs are being implemented in numerous schools in the Basque Country, and considering the positive effects they generate, we hope in the future they will become even more widespread.

In recent years, developed countries have shown a growing concern and social interest in connection with school violence and violence in general (gender, family, racist). This interest is also evident in the broad informational center of attention that the media are assigning to the topic of violence and, as a result of all this, research on violence has increased. Everywhere, at national and international levels, school violence has been verified to occur without noticeable differences in terms of geographical, cultural, or educational setting. All studies, without exception, demonstrate the existence of school violence; leading to the conclusion that this is a reality of school-life in general.

Although the positive role that these cooperative game experiences can bring about within the educational setting has been emphasized, education for social interaction should not only involve the school but also the family and society. For a social interaction plan to work, to raise supportive, egalitarian, peaceful, and tolerant children, everyone must participate: students, teachers, schools, and families. As the Maasai wisely say, "the full tribe is needed to educate a child," thus emphasizing the important educational function of society as a whole. Educating for social interaction, educating on equality, educating on tolerance, educating on non-violence, has become an extremely important educational goal, with school and family being the privileged settings for carrying out this task.

References

Ballou, Kathryn Jeanne. 2001. "The Effects of a Drama Intervention on Communication Skills and Learning Attitudes of At-Risk Sixth Grade Students." *Dissertation Abstracts International Section A: Humanities and Social Sciences* 61, no.10-A: 3828.

Bay-Hinitz, April K., and Ginger R. Wilson. 2005. "A Cooperative Games Intervention for Aggressive Preschool Children." In *Empirically Based Play Interventions for Children,* ed. Linda A. Reddy, Tara M. Files-Hall, and Charles E. Schaefer. Washington, DC: American Psychological Association.

Beilinson, Jill Selver. 2003. "Facilitating Peer Group Entry in Kindergartners with Impairment in Social Communication." *Language, Speech, & Hearing Services in Schools* 34, no.2: 154–66.

Carlson, J. Matthew. 1999. "Cooperative Games: A Pathway to Improving Health." *Professional School Counseling* 2, no.3: 230–36.

Cheah, Charissa S.L, Larry J. Nelson, and Kenneth H. Rubin. 2001. "Nonsocial Play as a Risk Factor in Social and Emotional Development." In *Children in Play, Story, and School,* ed. Artin Goncu and Elisa L. Klein. New York: Guilford Press.

Dyson, Ben. 2001. "Cooperative Learning in an Elementary Physical Education Program." *Journal of Teaching in Physical Education* 20, no.3: 264–81.

Finlinson, Abbie Reynolds, Ann M. Berghout Austin, and Roxanne Pfister. 2000. "Cooperative Games and Children's Positive Behaviors." *Early Child Development and Care* 164: 29–40.

Gagnon, Sandra Glover, and Richard J. Nagle. 2004. "Relationships Between Peer Interactive Play and Social Competence in At-Risk Preschool Children." *Psychology in the Schools* 41, no.2: 173–89.

Garaigordobil, Maite. 1996. *Evaluación de una intervención psicoeducativa en sus efectos sobre la conducta prosocial y la creatividad.* Colección Premios Nacionales de Investigación No. 127. Madrid: Centro de Publicaciones del Ministerio de educación y Cultura.

———. 2003. *Programa Juego 8–10 años. Juegos cooperativos y creativos para grupos de niños de 8 a 10 años.* Madrid: Pirámide.

———. 2004. *Programa Juego 10–12 años. Juegos cooperativos y creativos para grupos de niños de 10 a 12 años.* Madrid: Pirámide.

———. 2005a. *Programa Juego 6–8 años. Juegos cooperativos y creativos para grupos de niños de 6 a 8 años.* Madrid: Pirámide.

———. 2005b. *Diseño y evaluación de un programa de intervención socioemocional para promover la conducta prosocial y prevenir la violencia.* Colección Premios Nacionales de Investigación No. 160. Madrid: Centro de Publicaciones del Ministerio de Educación y Ciencia.

———. 2007. *Programa Juego 4–6 años. Juegos cooperativos y creativos para grupos de niños de 4-6 años.* Madrid: Pirámide.

Mikami, Amori Yee, Margaret A. Boucher, and Keith Humphreys. 2005. "Prevention of Peer Rejection Through a Classroom-Level Intervention in Middle School." *Journal of Primary Prevention* 26, no.1: 5–23.

Miller, Monica Campbell, Nancy L. Cooke, David W. Test, and Richard White. 2003. "Effects of Friendship Circles on the social interactions of elementary age students with mild disabilities." *Journal of Behavioral Education* 12, no.3: 167–84.

Moore, Melisa, and Sandra Russ. 2008. "Follow-Up of a Pretend Play Intervention: Effects on Play, Creativity, and Emotional Processes in Children." *Creativity Research Journal* 20, no.4: 427–36.

Roseth, Cary J., David W. Johnson, and Roger T. Johnson. 2008. "Promoting Early Adolescents' Achievement and Peer Relationships: The Effects of Cooperative, Competitive, and Individualistic Goal Structures." *Psychological Bulletin* 134, no.2: 223–46.

Smith, Peter K. 2005. "A Child's Work: The Importance of Fantasy Play." *Infant and Child Development* 14, no.1: 103–4.

Zan, Betty, and Carolyn Hildebrandt. 2003. "First Graders' Interpersonal Understanding During Cooperative and Competitive Games." *Early Education and Development* 14, no.4: 397–410.

4

Socialization to Prevent Gender Violence in the Basque Country

MARIA JOSÉ ALONSO OLEA, AITOR GÓMEZ GONZÁLEZ, and NEKANE BELOKI ARIZTI

In this chapter, we study preventive educational practices that address gender violence in the Basque Country, taking into account all the factors that have some bearing on socialization processes in children. These include steps aimed at teachers, students, relatives, and the rest of the educational community; with some of these activities being jointly executed.

The prevention of gender violence is a priority in many schools in the Basque Country. Various types of activities are underway that contribute to learning about and identifying gender violence. Some of these activities are instructional in nature, while others are more theoretical in nature and explore gender violence prevention in depth.

Through the Learning Communities project, schools have established mechanisms for preventative and proactive approaches to combat gender violence using *dialogue* or *community* conflict-prevention model. In this model, the entire community becomes involved in generating rules by consensus through egalitarian dialogue, and in their subsequent application. This process makes it possible to find the causes and sources of conflicts and the most appropriate solutions. Some of the schools applying this model have directly addressed matters related to preventing gender violence.

Aware that gender violence is a social problem, and that socialization is a key solution, various parties and institutions responsible for gender-based educational policies are working on training programs aimed at teachers, families, and other education stakeholders. There has also been important output of documents and materials intended to guide education professionals as they seek to prevent and overcome gender violence.

The Theoretical Basis

Academic research and literature contains many examples that show how gender violence affects women of various age groups, cultures, and academic levels. Murray A. Strauss (2004), verified, among other matters, that practically one third of university students had assaulted their partner during some dating situation within the twelve months prior to his survey. Indeed, there is a concern due to the numerous cases of sexual aggression against women in various university settings (Gross et al. 2006).

Gender violence problems have also been detected in elementary and in secondary schools. Several studies indicate a concern in connection with sexual assaults in dating situations and also in school settings (Silverman et al. 2001; Lavoie, Robitaille, and Hèbert 2000). Some authors such as Barrie Bondurant (2001) focus their attention on how the development of educational and prevention programs has positive implications in terms of communicating to women their lack of guilt for the assaults they suffer. Others, such as Wendy B. Charkow and Eileen S. Nelson (2000), are involved in analyzing research focused on the prevention of emotional-sexual relationships based on abuse and dependencies.

Because sexual aggression cases already exist in elementary schools, it is necessary to apply preventive measures. In this regard, we find contributions highlighting the importance of stereotypes and false beliefs in gender violence situations (Valls et al. 2007) that, especially in the case of youth, can lead them to confuse psychologically aggressive behaviors with affectionate behaviors (Cantera, Estébanez, and Vázquez 2009). Other contributions are committed to gender violence preventive socialization (Gómez 2004).

In the Learning Communities education project (Elboj et al. 2002) work is taking place from a dialogical perspective for purposes of improving social interaction in schools. The Basque Country is the pioneer autonomous community in Spain in this effort, since the first schools initiating this work have been Basque (Jaussi 2002). These schools work from the standpoint of socialization preventive of gender violence, in other words, trying to establish behaviors that promote egalitarian relationships that in turn serve to prevent violent actions (Gómez 2004; Oliver and Valls 2004).

Jesús Gómez (2004, 142–56) points out three basic elements for structuring a gender violence prevention model: the feeling of being capable of changing reality, high expectations, and enthusiasm. He also proposes three types of basic skills for the purposes of establishing emotional-sexual relationships that move entirely away from violent dominance values: attraction, choice, and equality.

Attraction Skills

Attraction skills are related to the belief that love is social and not biological. Therefore, it can be changed. "Knowing that love is neither instinctive nor impulsive, it is not something that happens inevitably, nor does it strike like a lightning bolt: love is not spontaneous, even if it seems to be, and if we want it to be so" (Gómez 2004, 144).

Instead, the feeling of attraction a person feels toward another person depends on the process of socialization on which we have structured our preferences. If starting at an early age someone has followed a process of socialization that has involved being attracted to violent individuals, it would be most common to feel attraction toward that type of person. But the social being can be changed, attraction skills can be used in order to critically analyze what is happening, reject the attraction toward violent and negative factors, and empower positive elements.

Choice Skills

These would make it possible throughout life to learn to recognize what choices would lead either to equal or to dominant relationships. Jürgen Habermas (1981a; 1981b) argues that it would be a matter of differentiating between choices based on expectations of validity (the force of arguments) and expectations of power (the argument of force). When options are taken based on relationships of dominance there is no equality, and it is therefore much easier for gender violence to occur, because an imposition by force exists.

Equality Skills

These skills make it possible to identify relationships of dominance, and how they become internalized. We are not accustomed to equality-based relationships, but we have the ability to attain emotional-sexual relationships based on friendship, camaraderie, and equality, which lead to relationships based on love and passion.

The authors who study socialization as a preventive to gender violence and violence-based relationships (Gómez 2004; Oliver and Valls 2004; Valls, Puigvert, and Duque 2008; Duque 2006) point out as essential the involvement of all educational actors in the emotional-sexual education of children in elementary and secondary schools. Thus, it is necessary from an early age to work on the topics of attraction and desire; in other words, to reflect on and discuss the people we feel attracted to, why, where these feelings lead us to, and how to change them should they be negative.

In the next sections we will delve in greater depth on practices and experiences which, on the basis of previous work by Jesús Gómez (2004), follow along the area of socialization to prevent gender violence. In particular we will analyze the work done in the Learning Communities schools.

Experiences and Practices

For some years now in the Basque Country there has been a concern in terms of developing educational initiatives for gender violence prevention, on the part of various agencies and individuals responsible for guiding educational efforts in both formal and informal settings. This concern has been taking shape in terms of different types of experiences that include training education professionals, educational practices in classrooms and schools, and the process of preparing materials and resources for the educational efforts involved.

In this section we analyze experiences stemming from a structural interpretation of gender violence, and therefore clearly intended to influence the socialization of the youngest children. In this account we focus on the leading role of the different socialization agents involved in educational processes. These are educational experiences resulting from the cooperation between schools and families and society as a whole, because as María José Díaz Aguado (2005) observes, current social dynamics require the cooperation of these central institutions.

Community-based Model and Preventive Socialization

As we have stated, the entire educational community must participate in gender violence prevention. Therefore, training is essential for teachers, families, and the community. The main goal is to provide research knowledge to identify gender violence and transform the dominant relationship model. Activities vary and may include: handing out of informational brochures to students and their families, giving formal lectures, and holding informal workshops that enable brainstorming and public debate by students, their families, and teachers. This latter activity, in particular, enables the entire educational community to discuss in-depth a theme that they share and construct.

In addition, some schools have developed specific mechanisms for gender violence prevention. These mechanisms follow the dialogical or community-based model for conflict prevention and resolution (Valls 2005) that allows the entire educational community—through egalitarian dialogue (Freire 1996; Flecha 1997)—to generate and apply rules by consensus. These rules need to comply with certain conditions: it should be possible to reach a consensus on them notwithstanding the different points of view existing in the community; they must be related to children's lives; be regularly broken, but relating to a behavior that is possible to eliminate; have widespread social support; and finally, once the behavior relating to the rule is overcome at the school, they should become an example for society, families, teachers, and students.

The schools working along the lines of this model are members in the Basque Country of the Learning Communities network.[1] They have been developing this model in theory and in practice since 2006, in schools as well as in interschool workshops. These schools are convinced that learning is impossible unless it takes place in conjunction with educational efforts to improve social interaction.

This was the core idea that motivated the San Antonio de Etxebarri Center for Elementary and Childhood Education (Bizkaia province, henceforth Etxebarri; Vega and Sanchez-Beaskoetxea 2007) to develop its social interaction project. This school's experience has served as a point of reference for other schools and as basis for practical-theoretical reflection at the network's workshops in the Basque Country.

The teachers and families had often found it difficult to understand conflicts that came up without apparent cause, especially in playing or dining areas. In the analysis carried out in Learning Communities schools, certain situations of abuse became evident on the part of older children

---

1. Chapter 6 contains information in greater depth on this educational project.

toward the younger ones, but also of boys toward girls. Overall, the Etxebarri experience has shown that, when the entire educational community participates equally in analyzing the causes and origins of gender violence, it is preventable and gives rise to an atmosphere of support, communication, and mutual awareness and improves the school's overall social interaction.

The development of the dialogue-based model for conflict resolution follows an established procedure consisting of seven steps. In the first step, a consensus is reached as to a rule that complies with the conditions mentioned earlier. For this purpose, a joint committee for social interaction is established, consisting of teachers, family members, students, and other education stakeholders, with the responsibility of proposing a rule and establishing the procedures for its debate within the education community.

Once the rule has been proposed, work takes place with all school groups until a consensus is reached. For example, one of initial rules agreed to by consensus in one of these schools was: *That no child may be assaulted for being deemed weaker.* A turning point in this process came from students' comments, by specifying that the problem was abuse inflicted by the stronger ones, and not the manner of dressing (as had been suggested initially).

Having reached an agreement as to the rule, there is then outreach throughout the community: in classrooms, at delegates' assemblies, at meetings of parents and relatives, and at teachers' staff meetings. Dialogue has always been important in terms of reviewing which dynamics facilitate rule compliance, and which ones interfere with it. Subsequent to this outreach phase, the students—with the support of the commission and of some tutors—are responsible for implementing and applying the rule. The students themselves present the result of their debate to meetings of parents and relatives and to their teachers. With input from the various groups, rules are implemented, as well as resolutions for applying them. Resolutions such as "offenses are not excusable" or "make the harassers openly known and confront them" are examples that show a way of addressing relationships between children based on respecting one's peers and not consenting to any form of violence.

Concurrently, training is organized for teachers and families. This training is essential for reaching a common understanding and sharing the rule's intent and significance. Thus, informal workshops take place with teachers, families, and students. Literature offers good opportunities to debate and brainstorm on values, while facilitating multiple avenues for learning. In addition, these workshops are settings where families, students, and teachers can participate jointly. The experiences that have taken place in these schools have been very positive in terms of better understanding the situations others are in, and for improving communication and social interaction. Moreover, when these workshops include relatives and students, there is an improvement in communications within the families themselves, and it encourages their participation in other community-based activities.

This entire process of rule formulation, implementation, dissemination, and application, aims primarily at having the entire community involved and committed to following and complying with the rule. The process itself, based on dialogue and consensus, provides a voice and a leading role to the students, makes it possible for all members of the community to share roles in decision-making and training, and creates in the schools an atmosphere that considerably improves social interaction. These are all important elements in the process of socialization for the prevention of gender violence.

In the development of the proposal, several points have been noted in the process of debate, reflection, and decision-making results. Teachers have become aware of harassment situations they had been previously oblivious to. It has also been seen that children are not passive observers, but are capable of facing situations they deem unfair and identifying their own abusive or violent behaviors. Debates between relatives and staff gradually stop being centered on attackers and those attacked ("my child could not have done that") with changes being introduced that make the school safer for all children. This process has enabled students as well as relatives to express situations of violence (harassment or abuse for example) in an atmosphere conducive to dialogue and to working in small groups.

Moreover, implementation of this dialogue-based model for conflict resolution makes it possible to reinforce various emotional-sexual education programs that were already underway in some of these schools. Some have taken place in cooperation with the Social-Educational Intervention Team (*Equipo de Intervención Socioeducativo*; EISE; *Gizarte eta Hezkuntza*

Eskuhartze-Taldea: GHEL)[2] from their municipalities, and others within the framework of the Nahiko program of Emakunde (Basque Women's Institute), which will be mentioned in a later section. We will specifically discuss the program carried out by the EISE-GHEL of Etxebarri, since it has one of the longer histories and is a pioneer Learning Community.

The program has been underway since 2000, and it involves the social educator as well as the group tutor. It addresses fifth and sixth grade elementary school students, and prior to its implementation in the classrooms the social educator holds an informational meeting with the families. Goals relate to the physiological, relational, and social aspects of sexuality, in order to clarify doubts, dispel myths, recognize one another as individuals, and respect and accept those who are different.

Methodology is based on dialogue. Participants put forth a situation for discussion, and at times supporting materials are used, such as comics or film. The experience developed reveals the existence of traditional socialization models, as described by one social educator:

> Responses from girls as well as from guys are really conservative: virginity is greatly valued, enjoying sex is a man's thing, they can have sex with many women, but it is frowned upon in the case of women. On this basis, I believe this type of social-educational programs help with gender violence prevention. Behind the thoughts expressed by the children there are justifications for chauvinistic and possessive behaviors that *dehumanize women* and that at a given moment culminate with actions included under "gender violence." Thus, settings need to exist for minors and youth to reflect, where adult facilitators can engage them in the task of analyzing these mindsets and behaviors surrounding relationships between men and women.[3]

In fact, the community-based model of social interaction promotes the development of these settings for reflection and analysis of the causes of violence, together with values that form the basis of a more fair and egalitarian relationship between all members of a community.

---

2. Social-Educational Intervention Teams are part of the Basic Social Services in the municipalities of Bizkaia. They work with minors and their families where there is a slight or moderate level of insufficient protection. They are governed by the "Plan for Social-Educational Intervention with Early Childhood, Youth and Family," Regional Decree 124/96 on December 17, from the Regional Government of Bizkaia. See Haurbabesa Lanbide Group (2009).

3. Interview with the social educator of EISE-GHEL of Etxebarri (Bizkaia) on January 15, 2010.

Some Key Factors: Continuing Development and Specific Didactic Materials

As we have seen, research and educational practices that can overcome inequities demonstrate the need for gender violence preventive socialization from an early age. However, one should not forget that even those who are charged with training are socialized through models based on inequality between genders, and imbalance in roles and relationships of power. Therefore, there is evidently a need to structure educational and social training for all those who are responsible for overseeing the socialization of minors and youth. These processes should be conducive to reflecting on the causes of gender violence; the values, beliefs, and concepts that support it; and should generate educational proposals guided by the concept of justice and equity. It is also useful to have available didactic materials intended not only for the classroom, but also for other contexts (family, spare time, leisure activities).

Training Educators

Preventive socialization is impossible without providing training to be responsible adults, and thus various groups and institutions in the Basque Country are carrying out various training initiatives. These are aimed at helping teachers, families, and educators review their knowledge and beliefs that reproduce androcentric roles and models, and contrast them against structured academic knowledge. The aim is to create coeducational initiatives that prevent gender violence in schools and the community.

The Basque government's Department of Education, Universities, and Research (hereafter DEUR), in the form of "School Training," has developed a ten-hour module that will initially be implemented at three schools selected from each of the educational networks existing in the Basque Country: public, private, and the ikastola system. The module is called "Education for Equality and for the Prevention of Gender Violence."

The purpose of this module is to provide settings and tools for debate and reflection that will encourage the educational community to carry out an integrated intervention. Its focus is equality and gender violence prevention. Therefore, although the module is initially implemented with teachers, it is also offered to families because the momentum of the entire educational community is needed for changes and improvements that will overcome inequality.

It is worth pointing out that different parties responsible for innovative programs (coeducation, social interaction, multicultural, Learning Communities) have participated in designing the module, with advisory services provided by researchers from the SAFO group (CREA, University of Barcelona).[4] In addition, prior to its implementation in schools, work has taken place with the technical assistance of the Berritzegunes[5] in charge of its support. The design itself is set forth as interdepartmental and interdisciplinary, cutting across all programs promoted by the Office of Educational Innovation of the DEUR.

It is also understood that this training must have an impact in schools, since the goal of equality requires including coeducation and gender violence prevention, in the curriculum, not as a one-time or occasional item—"tourist curriculum" (Torres 2001)—but as core curriculum and involving the entire educational community. Therefore, the module includes a reflection on how the school contributes to the persistence or to the transformation of sexist roles, and discusses sexist violence in general, paying special attention to the relationships of adolescents and youth. With these reflections as a starting point, an analysis is made on how coeducational initiatives in schools can contribute to the development of people's social skills.

In addition, the Continuing Development Program for Teachers offers a course titled "Coeducation: New Challenges." This course has four main goals for participants: To learn about the latest academic contributions from international research, and the best practices for overcoming gender violence, as well as contributions and barriers to feminism and feminist movements in educational practice. Identify gender violence at the school and existing barriers that must be overcome. Reflect on the importance of interactions in the transformation of gender relationships and identifying new social interactions between cultures that must be considered in a coeducational setting. And, finally, to prepare coeducational initiatives for gender violence prevention for their schools.

---

4. SAFO is the group for research on Women, from the CREA (University of Barcelona Center for Research on Theories and Practices for Overcoming Inequities).

5. Berritzegune: Support Center for Training and Educational Innovation; under the Office of Educational Innovation, Basque Government's DEUR.

In the same program, Adarra (the Movement for Pedagogical Renewal in Euskadi)[6] offers teachers a course titled "Emotional Sexual Education and Coeducation," which is also intended to encourage reflection on the basis of academic contributions and to debate educational proposals that encourage a change in the emotional relationships between minors and advance toward transformative coeducational practices.

Furthermore, Adarra has organized various symposiums addressing professionals in the field of education, university students, and other social and educational actors. In 2007, the symposiums were centered on "preventing mistreatment of girls and women," and in 2009 the work was based on "educating to eradicate sexist violence," with both having considerable repercussion in the specific educational and wider social environment.

The methodology is based on reflection and in constructing knowledge through dialogue (Arandia, Alonso-Olea, and Martínez-Domínguez 2010). A common procedure consists of informal workshops (Alonso-Olea, Arandia, and Loza 2008) with visual as well as written texts, which include the theoretical and scientific basis for socialization to prevent gender violence, and provides outreach regarding applicable rules and legislation. In the informal workshops, female teachers or mothers who considered themselves feminists, discover that they display behaviors that thwart the transformation of relationships between boys and girls. In other words, they discover how their own socializing process is sometimes a barrier in the transformation they wish to promote in gender relationships to achieve a more egalitarian and fair society. This debate on concepts, theories, and research leads to educational proposals and raises the question of how to implement them.

Therefore, the training of educational, family, and social professionals is an essential task. The same is true in the case of future education professionals who have been socialized within a cultural context that reproduces male and female intimacy models that reflect a structure of male dominance, and who reflect those values and attitudes in their own relationships (Amurrio et al. 2008). For this reason, some centers at the Universidad del País Vasco/Euskal Herriko Unibertsitatea (UPV/EHU,

---

6. Findings from the symposiums can be consulted, in Spanish and Basque, at: www.adarra. org.

University of the Basque Country) have been developing training efforts focused on preventive socialization, but they have been limited in scope.

In addition to proper training, it is also imperative to have resources and support available, since what is usually available to teachers and families consists of sex education materials, which are insufficient to address the skills of attraction, selection, and equality. Therefore, in the following section we reference those resources, materials, and programs that can help develop these skills in children and adolescents.

Materials for Preventive Socialization

Many different institutions and agencies have prepared materials for the prevention of gender violence. In this section, we will focus on two specific examples, because they explicitly deal with socialization to prevent gender violence. These materials consist, first, of instructional units directed toward the students, teachers, and families, developed by Emakunde within the Nahiko program, and second, the *Disconnect Yourself from Mistreatment* handbook, prepared by the Service for Attention to Women, Psychosocial Module of Deusto and San Inazio (Bilbao city hall, Bizkaia).

The Nahiko program's goal is to work within a coeducational framework for the prevention of violence against women (Emakunde 2003). It understands gender violence as a complex and multifaceted phenomenon rooted in the structural situation of inequality that women find themselves within society. Therefore, eradicating the problem requires coordinated steps in both the realms of intervention and prevention. All institutions and mechanisms that participate in the socialization process must work together to modify gender stereotypes and roles, and to foster values and models based on respect and equality.

Thus, it is a program for preventing abuse in the future relationships of students, initially addressing elementary education (ages six through twelve), and based on joint testing, research, and action with participating teachers and schools.

It is structured along three basic lines: training teachers, creating awareness in students and families, and developing materials. Within this framework, a series of curricular units has been developed in order to work with students, families, and teachers in the selected schools. The instructional units are structured for the third, fourth, fifth, and sixth grades in elementary schools (the intent is to also work with secondary students, although for the time being only experimental materials exist) and contain six modules: (1) human beings: care and commitment; (2) individuals: diversity and plurality; (3) equality: human rights; (4) trades and professions: the labor market; (5) the media: narrative and social success; and (6) social interaction with equality. Each consists of theoretical documentation surrounding the issue in question, instructor handbooks, notebooks for students as well as for families, and varied instructional material for working in training sessions. Student sessions are structured around various workshops where the methodology most commonly used consists of games.

With families, two training sessions take place per academic year: one at the beginning in order to inform the families of the work that will be done with the students throughout the school year, emphasizing the importance of the social-cultural model when analyzing and working on the prevention of gender violence; and another session at the end of the school year, in order to share with families the work done and to analyze its influence both in school and at home. An evaluation of the work sessions involving the students is then submitted to the families to reflect and work on the findings gathered. At the same time, four training sessions take place with teachers throughout the school year. These are aimed at offering training related to coeducation and for follow-up.

Specifically during one school year, a seminar took place with teachers who were working with these materials in order to facilitate their proper use with experts on their implementation.

It is also worth pointing out the *Disconnect from Mistreatment* handbook. This handbook is the result of research mentioned earlier by Itziar Cantera, Ianire Estebanez, and Norma Vázquez (2009). It is aimed at youth, intended to clarify concepts and confusion regarding love and violence, improve the acknowledgment of psychological violent behaviors, and provide some guidelines for proper mutual treatment in relationships. The guidebook follows the style of youth-oriented magazines, and includes various sections: comics, tests, a question and answer column, many pictures and illustrations, and most importantly, content on which to reflect, generate opinions, and share. In the words of the authors, it is "a guidebook so that girls and boys know how to treat each other well" (Cantera and Estebanez 2009). Unlike other materials aimed exclusively at schools, this guidebook is available from various bookstores for anyone who is interested. Within this same project, a blog has been started: "My boyfriend controls me . . . which is normal," ("*Mi novio me controla . . . lo normal*" at http://minoviomecontrola.blogspot.com/) in order to collect images and materials regarding youth gender violence, to show that it is a problem affecting even the youngest children, and finally, to foster egalitarian relationships between men and women.

Conclusion

Gender violence is a constant social problem. A report published by Emakunde titled *Violence against Women* (2009), reveals an increase of gender violence in the Basque Country. Likewise, another study by Emakunde, *Coeducation in the Basque Autonomous Community*, found that notwithstanding efforts made, the development of coeducation in the Basque Country has not been entirely satisfactory (2005, 149). Youth continue socializing within a culture that maintains the more traditional male and female role models, and that links attraction with violence.

Socialization to prevent gender violence proposes educational action based on developing the skills of attraction, selection, and equality, advancing toward an egalitarian relationship model. This is educational action that needs the commitment of the entire community, because the causes of violence must be analyzed from the actual settings of social and educational relationships, to be able to transform them.

The dialogue-based model for conflict resolution is an educational initiative in schools and communities that overcomes the limitations of other types of educational projects and promotes processes of gender violence preventive socialization. The experiences developed in the Learning Communities schools in the Basque Country are proving that progress is possible in this direction, as long as community involvement is present.

Being aware of this, various responsible parties from the DEUR have been working in the development of a base document in order to prepare a Plan for Coeducation and Prevention of Gender Violence, aimed at schools. Various social and educational institutions concerned and/or responsible for this matter have been involved in the development of this text. One should remember that in our information society learning takes place through interaction with different individuals, in each and every one of the frames of reference we move through. Therefore, continuity between these frames is essential, as is shown by increasingly more research (Aubert et al. 2004; Aubert et al. 2008).

The need for this comprehensive plan appears to be clear, resulting from consensus between various social and educational actors, to help advance toward equality between men and women. This means a plan that provides the momentum in schools so that coeducational projects can assist and contribute to the development of efforts preventing future inequality between men and women. And for this to happen, it is necessary to incorporate the work for equality into the whole curriculum, and to have families and other social agents participate equally. This participation must be supported by training processes, helping people introduce improved educational processes based on academic research, dialogue, and agreement. The experiences included in this chapter show that this type of education is possible and that it is already successfully underway.

References

Alonso-Olea, Maria José, Maite Arandia, and Miguel Loza. 2008. "La tertulia como estrategia metodológica en la formación continua: avanzando en las dinámicas dialógicas." *REIFOP* 11, no. 1 *(1)*. April 10. At www.aufop.com/aufop/home/.

Amurrio, Mila, Ane Larrinaga, Elisa Usategui, and Ana Irene del Valle. 2008. *Informe de investigación sobre Violencia de Género en las relaciones de pareja de adolescentes y jóvenes de Bilbao.* Bilbao: Ayuntamiento de Bilbao. November 18. At www.bilbao.net/nuevobilbao/ jsp/bilbao/pwegb010.jsp?idioma=C&color=rojo&textarea=DV9&s ubtema=10&padresub=D42&tema=D42&padre=*VD. (last accesed December 28, 2009).

Arandia, Maite, Maria José Alonso-Olea, and Isabel Martínez-Domínguez. 2010. "La metodología dialógica en las aulas universitarias." *Revista de Educación* 351 (April): 75–95.

Aubert, Adriana, Ainhoa Flecha, Carme García, Ramón Flecha, and Sandra Racionero. 2008. *Aprendizaje dialógico en la sociedad de la información.* Barcelona: Hipatia.

Aubert, Adriana, Elena Duque, Montserrat Fisas, and Rosa Valls. 2004. *Dialogar y transformar. Pedagogía crítica del siglo XXI.* Barcelona: GRAO Ediciones.

Bondurant, Barrie. 2001. "University Women's Acknowledgment of Rape: Individual, Situational and Social Factors." *Violence Against Women* 7, no. 3: 294–314.

Cantera, Itziar, and Janire Estebanez. 2009. "Mi nvio m kntrla l norml." *Blogspot.* April 4. At minoviomecontrola.blogspot.com.

Cantera, Itziar, Ianire Estébanez, and Norma Vázquez. 2009. *Violencia contra las mujeres jóvenes: La violencia psicológica en las relaciones de noviazgo.* Bilbao: Publicaciones del Gobierno Vasco; Emakunde; BBK.

Charkow, Wendy B., and Eileen S. Nelson. 2000. "Relationship Dependency, Dating Violence and Scripts of Female College Students." *Journal Of College Counselling* 3, no. 1: 17–28.

Díaz-Aguado, Maria José. 2005. "Aprendizaje cooperativo y prevención de la violencia." *Milenio. Revista Digital*: 5-15. At www.gh.profes. net/especiales2.asp?id_contenido=40431.

Duque, Elena. 2006. *Aprendiendo para el amor o para la violencia. Las relaciones en las discotecas.* Barcelona: El Roure.

Elboj, Carmen, Ignasi Puigdellivol, Marta Soler, and Rosa Valls. 2002. *Comunidades de Aprendizaje. Transformar la educación.* Barcelona: GRAO.

Emakunde (Instituto Vasco de la Mujer). 2005. *La Coeducación en la Comunidad Autónoma Vasca.* Informe, Emakunde y el Gobierno Vasco. Vitoria-Gasteiz: Publicaciones del Gobierno Vasco.

———. *Violencia contra las mujeres.* 2009. Informe, Emakunde y el Gobierno Vasco. Vitoria-Gasteiz: Publicaciones del Gobierno Vasco.

———. *Programa Nahiko.* January 10, 2003. At www.nahiko-emakunde. com/.

Flecha-García, Jose Ramón. 1997. *Compartiendo palabras. El aprendizaje de las personas adultas a través del diálogo.* Barcelona: Paidos.

Freire, Paulo. 1995. *A sombra desta mangueira.* Sao Paulo: Olho d'agua. English-language version: *Pedagogy of the Heart*, 1997, notes by Ana Maria Araújo Freire, translated by Donaldo Macedo and Alexandre Oliveira, foreword by Martin Carnoy, preface by Ladislau Dowbor. New York: Continuum.

Gómez, Jesús. 2004. *El amor en la sociedad del riesgo. Una tentativa educativa.* Barcelona: El Roure.

Gross, Alan. M., Andrea Winslett, Miguel Roberts, and Carol L. Gohm. 2006. "An Examination of Sexual Violence Against College Women." *Violence Against Women* 12, no. 3: 288–300.

Grupo Haurbabesa Lanbide. 2009. "El contexto institucional de la práctica profesional sobre infancia en desprotección en los tres territorios de la Comunidad Autónoma Vasca." *Revista Española de Educación Comparada* 15: 215–49.

Habermas, Jürgen. 1981. *Theorie des kommunikativen Handelns. Band I. Handlungsrationalität und gesellschaftliche Rationalisierung,.* Vol. 1. Frankfurt: Suhrkamp Verlag, 1981.

———. 1981. *Theorie des kommunikativen Handlens. Band II. Zur Kritik der funktionalistischen Vernunft.* Vol. 2. Frankfurt: Suhrkamp Verlag. English-language translation: *The Theory of Communicative Action,* 1984, translated by Thomas McCarthy. 2 vols. Boston: Beacon Press.

Jaussi, Maria Luisa, coord. 2002. *Comunidades de Aprendizaje en Euskadi/ Euskadiko Ikaskuntza Komunitateak.* Vitoria-Gasteiz: Servicio Central de Publicaciones del Gobierno Vasco.

Lavoie, Francine, Line Robitaille, and Martine Hèbert. 2000. "Teen Dating Relationships and Aggression: An Exploratory Study." *Violence Against Women* 6, no. 1: 6–36.

Oliver, Esther, and Rosa Valls. 2004. *Violencia de género. Investigaciones sobre quienes, por qué y cómo superarlas.* Barcelona: El Roure.

Silverman, Jay G., Anita Raj, Lorelei A. Mucci, and Jeanne E. Hathaway. 2001. "Dating Violence Against Adolescent Girls and Associated Substance Use, Unhealthy Weight Control, Sexual Risk Behavior, Pregnancy and Suicidality." *Journal American Medical Association* 286, no. 5: 572–79.

Straus, Murray A. 2004. "Prevalence of violence against dating partners by male and female university students woldwide." *Violence Against Women* 10, no. 7: 790–811.

Torres, Xurjo. 1994. *Globalización e Interdisciplinariedad. El curriculum integrado.* Madrid, Madrid: Morata.

Valls, Rosa, Lidia Puigvert, and Elena Duque. 2008. "Gender Violence Amongst Teenagers." *Violence Against Women* 14, no. 7: 759–85.

Valls, Rosa, Montserrat Sanchez-Aroca, Laura Ruiz-Eugenio, and Patricia Melgar. 2007. "¿Violencia de género también en las universidades? Investigaciones al respecto." *Revista e Investigación Educativa. RIE* (AIDIPE) 25, no. 1: 219–31.

Valls, Rosa. 2005. "Conveniencias y controversias en torno a la mediación intercultural." Primeras Jornadas de Mediación Intercultural en Canarias, La Laguna, December 12.

Vega, Carmen, and Marta Sanchez-Beaskoetxea. 2007. "Proyecto de convivencia de San Antonio ikastetxea publikoa." *Red de Comunidades de Aprendizaje*, September 30. At utopiadream.info/red/tiki-list_ file_gallery.php.

5

Resolution and Transformation of At-School Conflicts

Ramón Alzate Sáez de Heredia, Lucía Gorbeña,
and Cristina Merino

Students get into a fight during recess, someone shoves someone else who has tried to cut in line, or people respond with insults to derogatory comments about their work; these "incidents" appear to be the most natural thing in the world, given how frequently and steadily they are repeated. This behavior is so typical that it is often overlooked and people believe there is no conflict in schools. Everything happens as if frequency would standardize an initially undesirable situation. This reaches a point only when the level of conflict surpasses the limits of what is considered customary, the alarm is triggered, and the situation is deemed as "problematic."

If a comparison is made between how schools treat the reality known as "interpersonal relations," and how the areas known as "basic knowledge" and "the physical world" are treated, the comparative wrong is evident. No one doubts that curricular contents evolve with time, because they are the focus of a systematic learning process that begins at the earliest levels of schooling. Surprisingly, when it comes to knowledge pertaining to the world of interpersonal relations, the prevailing attitude makes it appear as if it were unnecessary to organize and systematize the matters to be learned, as if the knowledge was to be acquired at random or through spontaneous maturing. The idea that if one engages in educating for social interaction there will be no time left to teach content is wrong. Clearly, in order to teach content a school atmosphere needs to exist that makes it possible to approach the learning process under optimum conditions.

This type of school atmosphere grows day by day, with each small event that takes place.

But what does social interaction involve? Here is the definition and approach by Carlos Jiménez Romero:

> Social interaction is one of the terms most often used today by different individuals and social agencies, when it comes to stating what they hope to attain, or what they wish, what they are fighting for, what is the purpose of their actions in terms of group effort or mainstreaming, how societies should be, etc. This term always carries a positive connotation and is loaded with expectations, planning, seeking. . . . If coexistence is a given, social interaction requires laying a groundwork; this involves among other things, the learning process, tolerance, common rules, and regulating conflict. The most notable element in social interaction as an action, as interaction, is acknowledging that social interaction requires learning. Social interaction is an art that must be learned: "you need to learn how to socially interact with others," goes the advice. Social interaction involves two or more individuals or groups that are different, in a relationship where others always come into play, and is constantly being subject to change. It is often said that "social interaction is very difficult." It requires adapting to others and to the situation, being flexible. (2005, 8)

Social interaction requires tolerance, not in the sense of a patronizing gracious concession and showing compassion toward the one being dominated, but in the sense of accepting that which is different. An intolerant attitude is in conflict with the development of harmonious relationships or social interaction, because the other party is being rejected, either entirely or in certain elements essential to the relationship's life.

Social interaction also requires establishing certain common rules, commonly known as "rules for social interaction." Social interaction in a relationship not only emphasizes respect and tolerance of what is special, different, or opposite in the other party, but also highlights common grounds, points of convergence: a setting, social regulation of time, certain responsibilities, and the use of given resources. All this requires working out and agreeing on rules of engagement, accepted and followed by all.

Social interaction is not the opposite of conflict, nor does it mean lack of conflict, but it does require peaceful control or resolution of conflicts. We should make a record here of interpretations that perceive social interaction as a mere adaptation and accommodation without resolving the conflict. When dealing with the term "accommodation," Nicholas

Abercrombie, Stephen Hill, and Bryan S. Turner (1992, 17) define it as follows: "in the sociological analysis of ethnic relations, this term describes the process whereby individuals adapt to situations of ethnic conflict, without resolving the basic conflict or changing the underlying system of inequality. The term derives from experimental psychology, where it denotes how individuals modify their activity to fit the requirements of the external social world."

For all these reasons, and going one step beyond, we believe it is essential to introduce in schools programs for conflict resolution education (CRE). These programs can help schools transform their cultures by having them include a search for cooperative and peaceful solutions to conflicts and disputes, training in group problem-solving, shared decision-making, appreciating diversity, and developing a sense of community. In order to achieve these goals, comprehensive and global approaches must be undertaken that address conflict at the school from both a personal and structural perspective, as well as preparing students to face the future in a more peaceful, democratic, and fair society.

Of course we know that school, by itself, is insufficient for purposes of achieving this transformation and creating a peaceful society; but we also know that we have little chance for success in reducing violence, confrontation, and inequality if children and youth are not educated in the paths toward peace.

School Conflict Types and Social Interaction Problems

A classification is submitted that includes the different expressions of conflict in schools, not only in terms of violence and aggressiveness, but also those behaviors that impair learning and social interaction. This typology is merely methodological, considering that certain students can exhibit several of these behaviors. A student might demonstrate violent behavior, abuse and mistreat peers, and practice truancy, just to state an extreme example. Other students might show a lack of discipline toward actual classroom rules, without engaging in violent behavior toward their peers.

Breaches of Discipline

Multiple definitions exist for breaches of discipline in schools. Any given school's disciplinary system or regulatory code is the point of reference used to define the types of conflicts that constitute breaches of discipline.

Thus, behavior that violates the school's rules is considered a breach of discipline, no matter what those rules may be.

School regulations usually govern three major areas of school life: respect toward individuals, respect toward materials, and the management of academic and organizational aspects. Having made this distinction, it is worth pointing out examples of breaches of discipline in terms of each of the areas mentioned. Disrespect between students and teachers, aggression among students, and discrimination, are some examples of breaches of discipline in connection with respecting the individual. Breaking materials at school, stealing, or painting graffiti are examples of breaches of discipline involving respect toward materials. Tardiness, refusal to do homework, not bringing to class the necessary materials (books, notebooks, etc.), are examples of breach of discipline related to academic management and the way school life is organized.

Experts and teachers often consider breaches of discipline exclusively from the standpoint of the student as offender. However, other groups in the school community also commit violations of disciplinary systems, resulting in highly distortive social interaction problems at times. Thus, some teachers could at times exhibit tardiness, may be disrespectful toward students, or smoke in forbidden areas. Also parents sometimes violate school rules. For example, when a mother brings her three-year-old child to school with a fever, although this is forbidden because it puts other students at risk of contagion, she is also violating a school rule.

Disruption

Disruption refers to a range of behaviors that occur inside the classroom, aimed at obstructing or hindering the normal flow of the class. With assorted levels of intent, certain students decide to set up a boycott against the delivery of instruction, by generating commotion and engaging in other behaviors that elicit "warnings," thus impeding, interfering, or making it impossible to teach.

Disruption is the social interaction problem that typically causes the greatest concern for teachers and the least for students, since it is extremely stressful for the instructor and seriously interferes with his or her work. What is considered disruption or disruptive behavior depends to a great extent on each teacher's judgment. For example, some believe that chewing gum in class is unacceptable and distracting, while other instructors tolerate it. Therefore it is important, in terms of the appropriate response, for each school to reach a consensus among its members as to which behaviors are deemed disruptive and which are not.

Some examples of disruptive behaviors are: standing up in class without permission, wearing outlandish outfits, talking while the teacher is speaking, whispering to a classmate, taking things away from classmates, persistently asking questions with the intent to cause delays, making funny gestures, making derogatory comments about homework, asking to go to the restroom without reason, putting things away before its time without permission, challenging authority, not doing what should be done, getting into an argument with a classmate, insulting a classmate in class, throwing things around the classroom, and the list goes on.

Mistreatment between Peers

Mistreatment between peers is also known as harassment or bullying, and is a type of problem with great implications for social interaction at school, not so much from its impact or frequency, as from the consequences it can bring about in the individuals involved. Dan Olweus (1993, 54) defines mistreatment in the following terms: "A student is being bullied or victimized when he or she is exposed, repeatedly and over time, to negative actions on the part of one or more other students."

Other authors point out certain key features. According to María Victoria Trianes (1996), mistreatment between peers is an extended behavioral pattern consisting of social rejection, intimidation, and/or physical aggressiveness among the students themselves, who become victims of their classmates. According to Rosario Ortega Ruiz (2000) it is a matter of dominant-submissive relationships where certain students engage in abusive practices in order to subjugate and control others.

In all respects, situations of mistreatment involve a series of features that differentiate them from other types of conflicts or social interaction problems: A *power imbalance*, that is a disparity in physical, psychological, and social power, generating an imbalance of forces in interpersonal relationships. There is also *intent* and *repetition*, intent is expressed in an aggressive action that repeats over time and generates in the victim the expectation of being a target of future attacks. Finally, there are elements of *defenselessness* and *individualization*, where the target of the mistreatment is a single student, who is thus placed in a situation of defenselessness.

Mistreatment between peers tends to escape adult notice as it happens for the most part in their absence. In addition, there is an entire series of situations that adults sometimes perceive as "kids' stuff" or that are justified because "that's how it has always been," which nevertheless may be indicators of various types of mistreatment. Therefore, it is essential to be aware of the different modalities in which mistreatment can occur, so as to facilitate its identification.

Objecting to School

The levels of compulsory education vary from one country to another; in most, however, schooling is compulsory to a certain age. With this understanding, when education is compulsory until adolescence (ages fourteen to eighteen), there are students who create for themselves a life plan different from compulsory education; they no longer wish to be in school but remain there because they physically have to. Their resistant behavior's main feature is lack of motivation as far as schoolwork, and a self-evident refusal to learn or to devote any effort; they thus serve as negative role models for their classmates.

The profile of school objector is quite complex. Some of them come from unstructured families, from environments bordering poverty, or with deficiencies requiring a personal and specialized approach. In many cases, they exhibit behavioral problems and may become aggressive toward their classmates and teachers. However, there are also school objectors who are not violent, but arrive at school from undemanding family settings.

Truancy

Truancy, understood as the unauthorized nonattendance to class by a given student, does not necessarily involve the existence of a social or educational type of problem. Practically all adults can remember some instance during their school years when, for one reason or another, they decided to skip class without permission, without that absence having any major or negative repercussions on their educational process. However, when these absences happen repeatedly or occur along extended periods of time, the student's learning pace gets inevitably bent out of shape and academic delay problems begin to appear that, unless promptly resolved, can result in dropping out of school or failing. In these situations, truancy stops being a simple childish prank and becomes a serious educational problem.

Truancy makes itself evident in various stages: tardiness, absences from the first and last class period, intermittent absences from specific classes, sporadic absence from campus during regular school hours, and regular absence from campus. When it directly affects the student's educational process it should be considered a serious problem requiring intervention.

Truancy especially affects the most marginal segments of the population, and families that do not devote the necessary attention to their children's compulsory education. It is also the first step toward impoverishment and social exclusion. Thus, what at first is a simple educational problem, becomes in the medium or long term a serious social problem, and its treatment requires additional public resources.

Vandalism

These are serious behaviors, generally occurring outside of regular school hours. Vandalism breaches social rules and violates basic respect toward individuals and their properties. School vandalism is differentiated from some other aberrant behaviors in that it not only violates the school's regulations, but is also punishable by higher public authorities like the police. Some examples of school vandalism include arson, graffiti, breaking glass, and other types of destruction of a serious nature.

Interpersonal Conflicts

The school, as a place that various "communities" need to jointly inhabit on a daily basis, is a place where interpersonal conflicts happen frequently. Teachers, parents, students, administrators, and nonteaching staff interact, with education as their common aim. Nevertheless, they also have varied interests and goals that occasionally clash and result in conflicts quite varied in nature.

Interpersonal conflicts sometimes occur outside of the problems previously stated. Some interpersonal conflicts (such as two students arguing about a game) do not involve breach of discipline, disruption, or mistreatment between peers. It is, therefore, a broader category that may in turn include other problems among those mentioned. We will now examine the results of a study carried out to detect the social interaction situation and types of conflicts noted at a Basque Country public school.

Assessing Social Interaction and Conflict Conditions from the Students' Viewpoint

This questionnaire was answered by 154 students, 75 from lower secondary (ages twelve to fourteen) and 79 from upper secondary (ages fourteen to sixteen), with a classification margin of error in each group of plus or minus fifteen questionnaires.

Not all respondents answered every question in the questionnaire; therefore, percentages vary between some parameters. Nevertheless, the level of response is deemed sufficiently representative for purposes of visualizing the school's major needs in terms of handling day-to-day conflicts.

Both groups of students provided similar answers to the question as to whether conflicts interfere with the teaching and learning process. A majority (55.6 percent) believe that conflicts sometimes interfere with the learning process. In each of the groups surveyed, approximately 20 percent believe that this interference occurs frequently. The rest are of the opinion that this interference happens only in rare instances.

As far as the source of the problems, competitiveness or poor communications do not appear to be causes that generate problems. More than 80 percent of the responses state the opinion that only rarely or sometimes do conflicts take place due to either one of these two reasons. Results are similar in the case of intolerance between adults and students. Likewise, this intolerance does not appear to be a frequent cause of conflicts.

However, results vary when the students are asked whether problems exist that arise from intolerance among the students themselves. In this case, greater percentages reflected that these problems do occur frequently: an excess of 30 percent of the responses from students in lower secondary, and more than 20 percent of those from upper secondary.

Rumors appear to be one of the causes of greatest controversy among students, with the responses reflecting percentages similar to those referring to intolerance among students themselves. We should point out that the responses from lower secondary to the question "How frequently do problems arise from rumors?" are much greater than the responses from upper secondary; therefore, we have concluded that rumors cause greater concern in lower secondary than in upper secondary. Likewise, to a lesser extent in terms of frequency—usually—but greater when responding that it happens in "some instances," are the answers referring to anger and/or frustration and problems arising outside of school.

Therefore, we can conclude that students' perception in terms of what causes problems is substantiated in the first place by the intolerance taking place between themselves, second by the school rumors, which result in an atmosphere with higher levels of conflict in the classrooms, and third by the anger or frustration generated among the students.

The perception in terms of punishment varies significantly between the two groups. Students in lower secondary produce lower responses with regards to the frequency that punishments or warnings occur. The responses on punishment are higher in upper secondary students, thus leading to the conclusion that they receive a greater number of warnings than their counterparts in lower secondary.

The results are as follows: The highest percentages, with a mean of 36 percent among students in both lower and upper secondary, are in those responses that believe punishment is more frequent as a result of problems among students. However, only 20 percent believe that punishment is frequent when problems arise between students and instructors. This percentage reaches 46 percent when the opinion is that "sometimes" the punishment is indeed motivated by friction between students and teachers. Also significant is the perception of school regulations as a cause for punishment in students. More than 30 percent of the responses express the belief that punishment or warnings are often the result of problems arising between students and school rules. That this occurs "sometimes," is the opinion of 38 percent of respondents.

The next question the students were asked referred to the types and frequency of conflicts they themselves had experienced. First, we notice that brush-offs, insults, and "pulling someone's leg," occur with great frequency among the students, reflecting percentages very similar in both groups. It is significant that only 12 percent in lower secondary and 4 percent in upper secondary believe that these behaviors occur only rarely. Thus, a majority of the students surveyed (56 percent) believes that they happen frequently, and 35.5 percent said "sometimes." If we compare these figures with the results obtained from other similar schools, we can conclude that these are the types of conflicts that most often occur.

Threats between students are also a source of conflicts. From the responses, we have learned that in lower secondary there is a perception that threats are more frequent than in upper secondary. Taking the statistical mean of both groups, we notice that 40 percent of both groups believes that they occur frequently, and another 40 percent that they are less prevalent. Only 20 percent in both groups believes that threats between students are rare.

In terms of intolerance toward differences, slightly more than 30 percent of the students believe that conflicts often occur triggered by intolerant attitudes on the part of the students. Intolerance toward differences is greater in upper secondary than in lower secondary.

Loss of property does not generate, according to the students, a high percentage of school conflicts. Only 21 percent of the students believe that loss of property happens frequently, while 79 percent are of the opinion that this happens only in certain instances or rarely. Results are similar to those obtained regarding conflicts caused by access to groups.

In terms of conflicts stemming from rumors at school, some high percentages appear, in lower as well as upper secondary. In this regard, only 17 percent of the lower secondary students polled believe conflicts caused by rumors are rare, while 34 percent of the students from both groups belief that these conflicts happen frequently.

As far as physical fights, we find significant differences in both groups. Results from lower secondary show a high percentage of responses, 75 percent, indicating a belief that fights happen frequently or sometimes, while according to 25 percent they happen only rarely. On the other hand, in upper secondary there is a majority of responses to the effect that fights occur rarely or in some instances. This difference in the results could indicate that lower secondary is immersed within a timeframe when some physical fights are taking place among the students, resulting in a heightened perception of these fights as compared to upper secondary.

In the section on verbal harassment among students, results obtained are also high in both groups. More than 80 percent of the total students believe that these verbal fights happen frequently or sometimes.

Controversies resulting from schoolwork are not perceived as important by students completing the questionnaire, particularly those from lower secondary. These controversies rarely occur, in the opinion of 44 percent of these students. This percentage is slightly higher in upper secondary students who respond that conflicts do sometimes arise, although the percentage is not significant. Physical fights, verbal harassment, and rumors appeared to be the major sources of conflict in the schools we studied.

In terms of the effectiveness of actions or sanctions aimed at modifying problem behaviors, we notice that students perceive permanent expulsion as either very effective or somewhat effective for over 80 percent of the group in the sample. It is particularly significant that more than 50 percent of the responses in upper secondary are of the opinion that this step is very effective. It also seems significant that in lower secondary the opinion that it is not effective is more common in comparison with the responses from upper secondary.

The perception of this step's effectiveness is reduced when the expulsion is temporary. According to the group sampled, a temporary expulsion is only partially effective in terms of modifying problematic behaviors. From these two responses we conclude that students know that certain actions could get punished with a temporary or a final expulsion. The power of coercion and self-control is motivated to a greater extent by fear of this type of serious sanction, than by other possibilities.

In terms of the possible effectiveness of not engaging in any scheduled activities, such as visits, field trips, or extracurricular activities, we notice that for lower secondary this could entail an effective action for purposes of behavior modification. However, most responses from upper secondary believe that this is ineffective as a course of action.

The responses from both lower and upper secondary coincide in the belief that performing a additional activities or tasks is ineffective to modify problematic behaviors. In particular it is deemed ineffective in upper secondary, with an 80 percent of responses in this regard. On the other hand, being sent to the principal's office, complaints from teachers and parents, and most importantly, detention, are perceived by the sample as effective.

Thus, in both lower and upper secondary, 75 percent of the responses indicate that being sent to the principal can be very effective or somewhat effective. These percentages on perception of effectiveness increase considerably in connection with complaints from teachers or from the parents. Here almost 87 percent of the group sampled believes that these are somewhat effective or very effective courses of action.

Finally, detention, or being kept at the school after regular hours, is perceived as an effective course of action for purposes of modifying problematic conducts, particularly for lower secondary.

Next the questionnaire asks about the influence, in the broad sense, exerted by the different groups that constitute the education community, in terms of modifying school organization and operation.

In their replies, students in lower and upper secondary believe that the different groups in the education community exert certain power, or a great deal of it, when it comes to doing something to change the way the school operates. Responses reflect similar percentages in the power to modify school operations when referring to the students themselves, teachers, parents, principal, administrators, inspectors, delegates, and counselors. The perception, therefore, is that the education community consists of various constituencies, all of them with sufficient power to influence school organization and operations.

As to the perception of the treatment received by students, we see that lower secondary students believe that they are almost always treated with respect in 43 percent of the cases, compared to 58 percent in the responses from the upper secondary group. On the other hand, in 10 percent of the cases in both lower secondary and upper secondary, students believe they are almost never treated with respect.

We find similar percentages when facing the issues of being treated with appreciation and equal opportunities. In both cases, approximately 10 percent of the responses state that they are almost never treated with appreciation or with equal opportunities. In the responses, 62 percent affirm that they almost always feel accepted, whereas 7 percent believe that they are almost never accepted.

The response is significant when asked whether the students are treated with fairness at the school. Only 37 percent, as a mean in both lower and upper secondary, assert that they are almost always treated fairly; 45 percent believe they are only sometimes treated with fairness; and a 17 percent believe they almost never receive a fair treatment.

Of the students surveyed, 49 percent believe they are only sometimes allowed to solve the problems affecting them. They are almost always granted this opportunity according to 41 percent of the responses, and only 10 percent believe they are almost never allowed to do so.

When asked if the school should improve and teach students some type of conflict resolution skills, we find the following responses (average percentages were taken from both lower and upper secondary, since no significant differences appear in the responses from each group).

Most significantly, almost 60 percent of the sampling believes that techniques of anger control should definitely be taught. In the opinion of 32 percent the response is perhaps, and only 8 percent believe that there should definitely be no teachings on this issue. On the other hand, we also notice that 12 percent believe that there should definitely be no teachings on to how to express our feelings to others, with 31 percent believing the contrary, and a majority of 57 percent not following along the lines of either one of the two responses above.

Approximately 50 percent are of the belief that techniques should definitely be taught that would help learn how to deal with opinions, respecting authority, and ignoring those who deliberately annoy. Less than 10 percent believe there should be no efforts to work on these topics at school.

Finally, 57 percent of those queried believe the school should improve and teach how to solve problems that arise among students. In the opinion of 36 percent, perhaps the school should offer this information, and slightly more than 7 percent feel that the school should definitely not offer information on this matter.

Asked whether students request help when needed, we find in the group that 43 percent almost always ask for help, 47 percent do so sometimes, and 9 percent almost never ask for help. These percentages indicate that the group usually asks for help. We shall now see who is asked for help when it becomes necessary:

Students rely especially on parents and others students, and to a lesser extent on other family members. In the sample queried, 93 percent ask for help mostly from parents, with an 82 percent relying on other students, or a 65 percent that would trust some other family member, mainly siblings.

In terms of asking for help from teachers, numbers vary between lower and upper secondary. Thus, the percentage of respondents stating they would seek help from teachers is greater in lower secondary, with close to 80 percent of students who would ask for this help, whereas the percentage drops to 62 percent for students in upper secondary.

Figures related to seeking help from school guidance staff are significant. We find that a majority of the group sampled, 71 percent, would definitely not ask for help from the guidance staff, compared to a 20 percent who perhaps would request it, and 8 percent who would definitely request help from the guidance department. Other groups that students are less inclined to ask for help include other members of the school, or other adults.

Also significant are results referring to students' perception as to whether the school is particularly problematic. When asked if their school has more problems than the rest of the schools, 38 percent says yes, that we are at a school that is more problematic than the mean. Meanwhile, the school has more or less the same problems as the rest of the schools, according to 55 percent of the students, and only 6.6 percent of the group believes their school has fewer problems than the rest of the schools. Therefore, we find ourselves with the generalized perception among the students that they are at a school that is at least as problematic as other schools, if not more. This perception shows very similar percentages in both lower and upper secondary.

The last close-ended questions posed to the students refers to how school conflicts are solved between persons of different cultural origins. In this sense, the responses most often given state that these types of problems never get resolved, or else they do get resolved, but in an aggressive manner. This indicates a high level of prejudice toward differences. The second set of responses, in a slightly lower percentage, expresses the opinion that normally conflicts are resolved by means of dialogue, or it is the teachers who are in charge of solving those problems. According to a minimal percentage, only two responses, there are never problems at the school.

Proposal for an Education Program on Conflict Resolution/Transformation

If we want our teachings on conflict resolution to truly fulfill our goals and to achieve a significant change in the way students face their responsibilities, relationships, and conflicts in their daily lives, we will need to make adaptations to the school as an institution and to the principles and values underlying those teachings. This is not exclusively a curricular issue, but involves a systemic change to the school. The obstacles impeding the development of responsible behavior permeate the entire school structure and, therefore, the classroom structure. Attempts to change the instruction, unless accompanied by changes in the system—which ultimately allows these attempts to succeed or fail—will hardly produce the expected results.

All this can be addressed by what we call the comprehensive academic approach (*Enfoque Escolar Global*; Alzate 1998b, 1999b, 2000), which involves simultaneously implementing within the academic framework curricular programs on conflict resolution, mediation programs between classmates and peers, transformation of the pedagogical relationship, and intervention in the school atmosphere, as well as the commitment of the various key players, students, teachers, administration, and parents.

Principles and Goals

The true goal of CRE professionals is to contribute, through education, to a transformation in our society. Education programs that focus on "keeping the peace," preventing disruptions, and maintaining the control that "feels" lost, provide students with self-regulating capabilities, lasting "life" skills that help them become fair, democratic, and peaceful citizens. It is a transformation that can lead us, as has already been stated, from the culture of violence we currently live in to a culture of peace.

This position, advocated by conflict resolution professionals, reflects the principles and philosophy embedded in UN Resolution 53/25. This resolution, the "International Decade for a Culture of Peace and Non-Violence for the Children of the World, 2001–2010" (1995) and its preamble recognizes the role of education in constructing a culture of peace and nonviolence and emphasizes the creation of a culture of harmony, peace, and nonviolence that should emanate from adults and be instilled in children with the overall goal of strengthening international peace and cooperation.

In developing this declaration, a program of action was approved (1999), which in its section 9 "Actions to foster a culture of peace through education," it declares the need to:

> b. Ensure that children, from an early age, benefit from education on the values, attitudes, modes of behaviour and ways of life to enable them to resolve any dispute peacefully and in a spirit of respect for human dignity and of tolerance and non-discrimination;
>
> c. Involve children in activities designed to instill in them the values and goals of a culture of peace.[1]

The insoluble relationship between promoting a culture of peace and conflict resolution education is quite clear, because, to paraphrase Freud regarding dreams and the unconscious, we believe that peaceful conflict resolution is the noble path to a culture of peace. This is true to the extent that we believe, conceptually, a culture of peace should be understood not as a conflict-free utopia, but as a culture where individuals, groups, and nations interact cooperatively and productively between themselves,

---

1. United Nations General Assembly. Resolution 53/243 B. Programme of Action on a Culture of Peace. A/Res/53/243/B, September 13, 1999. At www.un-documents.net/a53r243b.htm.

and where conflicts, which inevitably arise, are handled in a constructive manner.

What Does CRE Mean?

CRE teaches and shapes in a culturally appropriate and evolutionally adjusted manner a variety of processes, practices, and skills designed to address individual, interpersonal, and institutional conflicts, and to create a receptive and secure educational atmosphere. These skills, concepts, and values help individuals understand conflict dynamics and enable them to use communication and creative thinking in order to build healthy relationships and to handle and resolve conflicts in a fair and nonviolent manner. Educators in the field of conflict resolution strive to achieve a fair and peaceful world, where citizens act in a responsible and civilized manner in their interactions and in their dispute resolution processes.

The main goal of CRE programs is to provide students with the skills necessary to solve conflicts nonviolently and by means of efficient communication, cooperative problem-solving, and the capability of taking a stand. Additional work must also be done in schools with teachers, administrative and support staff, and families.

Thus, we can see how from the final goal (transforming society), CRE creates specific proposals related to the daily social interaction of individuals and groups that underlie the process of promoting the culture of peace: educating for a culture of peace, educating for peace, and educating for social interaction and peace.

More specifically, CRE goals vary depending on the programs—or combination of programs—adopted. Five of the most common goals appear below (Jones and Kmitta 2000). Some programs focus on only one or two of these goals, while others attempt to address the entire set.

- Create a healthy atmosphere conducive to learning
- Create a constructive environment for learning
- Improve classroom management
- Reinforce students' social and emotional development
- Create a constructive community in the face of conflict

The All-encompassing Model for Social Interaction at School

During the fourth conference of the World Council for Curriculum and Instruction (Edmonton, Canada, 1984), one of the presentations suggested that although education tries to be nonpartisan, it cannot remain neutral when facing problems of justice and injustice, cooperation and dominance, or peace and violence. In education a choice must be made between socializing along the existing order, or else teaching that any social order can be modified (Chetkow-Yanoov 1996). In fact, schools have long socialized youth in attitudes deemed essential for adult citizenry; for this reason, they should steer their efforts toward preparing youth and adults for a nonviolent lifestyle within a framework of inclusivity.

There is an increasingly widespread belief that CRE and education for social interaction (terms that mean practically the same thing, so from this point on forward the first of the two will be used exclusively because of its international recognition), are necessary and appropriate at all levels of primary and secondary education. However, daily experience shows their failure when it comes to modifying attitudes and behavior, either in the short or long term. Why does this happen?

Most educators consider the principles of significance and relevance essential for academic achievement; for teaching to be effective and long-lasting, material and content must bear certain relevant connection with the experiences and interests of the students.[2] In our programs (Community Boards and Alzate 2000; Alzate 2000)—as in most other school conflict resolution programs—we have taken significance and relevance into account when designing activities aimed at developing pertinent skills in children and youth. Therefore, it is difficult to understand why we are sometimes not more successful despite our knowledge of the proper pedagogy.

If we want CRE to fulfill its goals and create a significant change in how students face their responsibilities, relationships, and conflicts in daily life, it is necessary to adapt the school as an institution to its underlying principles and values. This is not exclusively a curricular matter; it involves a system change by the school. As we have mentioned before, barriers impeding the development of more peaceful and cooperative behaviors permeate the whole school organization, and therefore permeate into classrooms. Significant changes in behavior are unlikely unless they occur together with structural changes.

---

2. See Cookson and Schneider (1995); Darling-Hammond (1997); DeVries and Zan (1994); Noddings (1992); and Sandy (2001).

This is addressed by the "all-encompassing school focus" (*enfoque escolar global*; Alzate 1998a). This approach simultaneously implements CRE curricular programs, peer mediation programs (Boqué 2003), pedagogical relationship transformations, and intervention in the school atmosphere. It also involves all of the key players: students, teachers, administrators, and parents.

All-encompassing Approach for School Conflict Transformation

The approach we advocate broadens the child-centered focus to include administrators, teachers, and parents. If we understand the controversies that occur among children and youth within the entire educational context, we begin to reach more meaningful solutions.

However, in conversation with many veteran teachers, they maintain that today's youth are increasingly undisciplined, involved in more conflicts dealing with more irrelevant issues, and are more violent. If we pay attention to recent media reports, they drink more, destroy public property, lack respect for others, and the list goes on. Overall, analyses and descriptions such as these—and the subsequent remedies proposed—are entirely youth focused. We might ban certain practices, toughen disciplinary codes, and so on—on the negative side—or otherwise educate, introduce corrective or counterbalancing programs, introduce CRE programs and mediation on the positive side. However, these kinds of problems are symptoms of a decayed society, not its cause. Consequently, without disregarding the symptoms, ideas (such as a culture of peace or a comprehensive focus) should be generated that focus on transforming causes to the extent possible.

The link between the child-centered CRE approaches (curriculum and mediation programs) and the all-encompassing ones is analogous to a pot of water that is brought to boiling point (Field 1996). A pot of boiling water can be represented pictorially as a source of heat, a series of small bubbles beneath the water's surface, and large boiling bubbles on the water's surface. School conflicts rise just as the bubbles do at boiling point, due to the "boiling" tensions among adults as well as among children, and between adults and children. Often certain underlying problems, such as defective communication or inefficient school policies, become the "heat source" responsible for the tensions. The person-centered approach for conflict resolution is reductionist, because it focuses almost exclusively on surface conflicts. The all-encompassing approach is much more comprehensive because if focuses on all three conflict parameters: the conflicts on the surface at "boiling point"; the boiling relationship tensions between adults as well as between students; and the "heat sources" underlying the conflict.

The relationship between both approaches can be analyzed from two different perspectives. Initially, a vertical top-down posture can be adopted, which would begin by treating conflicts specific to students. For example, to address a controversy between children involving physical aggression, the teacher must "react" in the face of the current "crisis," to make sure neither of the children is injured. Once the children have been calmed down and the current crisis resolved, connections would be sought between this argument—over Batman, for instance—and divided opinions among teachers regarding the appropriateness and value of playing with superheroes. When the link between these conflicts is established, the underlying cause of the different conflicts can be uncovered. According to the top-down perspective, children's conflicts are a window that allows us to discover underlying adult tensions and controversies.

Second, a bottom-up perspective can be adopted. This perspective is proactive, because the school is committed to establishing a general framework of serious conflict prevention. This framework is aimed toward facilitating and fostering positive relationships among students, parents, and teachers, as well as establishing consensual guidelines that minimize the general level of school conflict. According to this perspective, the Batman conflict could have been avoided if a clear guideline existed about bringing superhero toys to school. The conflict resolution goal according to this perspective is prevention.

As a consequence of applying these ideas, a new system is available for managing students' conflicts at school, which is represented by a pyramid shape in figure 5.1. At the base of the pyramid are potential conflicts that never occur due to an improved school environment, use of the curriculum, more effective classroom management, and a more democratic school structure. Second, most of the conflicts occurring could be solved by the students themselves using the learned skills of self-control, and cooperative problem-solving. Those problems that cannot be solved by the students themselves would go to a mediation process among peers or mediation by an adult. Finally, a small percentage of conflicts would be arbitrated by an adult.

Figure 5.1 The ideal system of conflict resolution

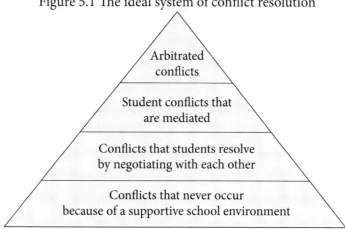

Source: Cohen 1995, 35.

Implementation of this all-encompassing model for conflict transformation at the school requires a sequence of medium-term steps for the gradual and coordinated implementation of its different elements.

Discussion and Findings

Studies evaluating the efficiency, usefulness, and limitations in the application of CRE programs are relatively recent; however, we are starting to have a good amount of well-executed research available.

Program Effectiveness

As a result of a symposium that took place in March 2000, a superb work was recently published titled *Does It Work? The Case for Conflict Resolution Education in Our Nation's Schools*, edited by Tricia S. Jones and Daniel Kmitta (2000). This work, in the analysis of existing evidence on the effectiveness of school CRE and mediation programs, sets forth five areas for analyzing the effects of the programs: CRE impacts on students, educators, overall school climate, and diverse groups of people, as well as the CRE's effects on institutional matters.

The research shows positive effects on students, particularly when CRE includes the entire school community: children, parents, educators, all levels of school staff, and the community. Many CRE efforts fail because implementation is narrowly focused and involves only students.

There is, however, insufficient follow-up research on students who have received two or three years of training in conflict resolution.

Very little formal research has studied the effects of CRE on educators. General findings on this topic arise from more general assessments of the CRE. Findings usually start from the number of conflicts or disciplinary problems that teachers report about their classes. It is assumed that those teachers who learn to teach conflict resolution to children are also developing skills for solving their own conflicts and modeling this conduct with their students, but little formal evidence supports this conjecture. Anecdotally, we have heard from teachers in teacher trainings about their efforts to apply CRE principles and techniques in their environments.

There is, however, research to support CRE as having a positive impact on classroom atmosphere. However, these studies have been criticized for lacking agreement as to the definition of "school atmosphere," and for needing more on-site information on the behavior as well as from longitudinal data.

Analysis has been made of factors inhibiting or enhancing institutionalization of CRE in school systems (Jones, Batton, and Carruthers 2000). In the National Curriculum Integration Project (Jones, Sanford, and Bodtker 2000), researchers developed integrated curricula and incorporated them into traditional curricula in seven middle schools at different locations. The assumption was that CRE should be considered as an integral part of the educational process if it is to be comprehensively institutionalized. However, this integration requires commitment, resources, and planning in order to sufficiently motivate teachers and administrators to achieve its total implementation.

Thus, the practical model for conflict resolution requires more time and commitment from everyone in the school system than what most educators currently believe to be feasible. Although many teachers, administrators, and other school staff are very aware of the need to totally integrate social-emotional learning and conflict resolution, they feel incapable of implementing programs.

In addition, many CRE activities encourage the group to share personal and possibly sensitive experiences regarding conflict or to express their deep emotions and thoughts. At the beginning, there is the risk that an activity could be too intense or that it may affect group cohesion, so an "ice breaker" that does not require a great deal of trust may be necessary.

Creating an atmosphere of trust is the main task when beginning a workshop or sequence of activities.

Limitations in Applying CRE Programs

There is a series of limitations that can hamper positive results when instituting school CRE programs. Here we focus on those that deal with the role of teachers exclusively (Alzate 2000).

Lack of CRE training in the traditional teacher education, along with the lack of sufficient time for internal teacher training impede the effective use of the curriculum. The most effective instructors are those with prior information, training, or knowledge on some topic related to interpersonal communication, affective education, or other similar matters. On the other hand, some teachers who have received a one-day training and feel satisfied with it nevertheless feel uncomfortable when it comes to teaching conflict resolution that they have had little if any opportunity to put it into practice.

Low levels of ease and comfort with CRE curriculum create a secondary problem; that is, the lack of consistency in CRE scheduling. This lack of consistency occurs between different classrooms at the school. Teachers vary in material, frequency of lessons, and time devoted to CRE teaching. Indeed, one study (Hancock, Pager, and Elias 1993) showed that consistency in school scheduling was an important factor in terms of teaching social skills.

Another problem specific to adults without prior CRE training arises from the lack of consistent modeling. In these situations, students receive mixed messages. It is a very common experience to hear upper secondary students ask why teachers don't practice what they preach, or why they force students to shoulder the responsibility for changing the way conflicts are handled. However, it is inadvisable to put too much emphasis on this aspect of adult modeling.

However, along the lines of what we consider a basic principle for the effectiveness of the CRE programs—instructors should serve as true models of the qualities and skills they are helping to develop in their students—it becomes necessary to generate changes in the instructors themselves as well as in their teaching styles. Accomplishing these changes involves new challenges in addition to the growing demands teachers face.

Issues for the Establishment of a Global CRE Program

A comprehensive approach to conflict and violence is a multiannual enterprise that needs the support of administrators and management. All groups working at the school must become an integral part of the project.

Plans for implementation must be carefully designed, whether for buses, dining rooms, schoolyards, or classrooms; or are aimed at adults or students. They also must be acceptable to all those involved.

Teachers need long-term support in order to learn CRE theory and practice, until they feel comfortable in its daily use with their colleagues and students. Any innovation in the education arena takes time to settle. Therefore, if we wish for the change to remain, new hires must be offered the training and tools that the rest of the staff already has. In sum, the overall effect of the CRE program on the school's environment depends on its all-encompassing integration and support.

References

Abercrombie, Nicholas, Stephen Hill, and Bryan S. Turner, *Diccionario de Sociología*. Madrid: Cátedra, 1992. English: *The Penguin Dictionary of Sociology*: London: Penguin, 1988.

Adams, David, ed. 1995. *Unesco and a Culture of Peace*. Paris: Unesco.

Alzate, Ramón. 1998a. "Los programas de resolución de conflictos en el ámbito escolar." *Organización y Gestión Educativa* 4: 14–18.

———. 1998b. "Resolución de conflictos en la escuela." *Ensayos y Experiencias* 24: 44–63.

———. 1999a. "Enfoque global de la escuela como marco de aplicación de los programas de Resolución de Conflictos." In *Mediación escolar. Propuestas reflexiones y experiencias*, edited by Florencia Brandoni. Buenos Aires: Piados.

———. 1999b. "Algunas reflexiones sobre la práctica de la mediación familiar." *Acord* 11: 1–3.

———. 2000. "Conflicto y Escuela." *Letras de Deusto* 87: 15–30.

———. 2003. "Resolución de conflictos. Transformación de la escuela." In *Aprender del conflicto. Conflictología y educación*, edited by Eduard Vinyamata. Barcelona: Graó.

———. 2006. "La mediación escolar. Proceso colaborativo de la educación en resolución de conflictos." *Trabajo Social Hoy*, Monográfico: 75–96.

———. 2008. "Programas de convivencia en el ámbito socioeducativo: Enfoque global de transformación de conflictos y mediación." *Proyecto Hombre* 66: 15–18.

Alzate, Ramón, Lucía Gorbeña, Amaia Aguirre, Cristina Merino, and Carlos Romera. 2002. "Aplicación de un programa escolar global de transformación de conflictos en la educación primaria." *Aula de Innovación Educativa* 115: 48–51.

Boqué, Mª Carme 2003. *Guía de mediación escolar. Programa comprensivo de actividades de 6 a 16 años.* Barcelona: Octaedro.

Brandoni, Florencia, ed. 1999. *Mediación escolar. Propuestas, reflexiones y experiencias.* Buenos Aires: Paidós.

Chetkow-Yanoov, Benyamin. 1996. "Conflict Resolution Skills Can Be Taught." *Peabody Journal of Education* 71, no. 3: 12–28.

Cohen, Richard. 1990. *Manual de Entrenamiento en Mediación Escolar.* Belmont, MA: School Mediation Associates.

———. 1999. *The School Mediator's Field Guide: Prejudice, Sexual Harassment, Large Groups and Other Daily Challenges.* Watertown, MA: School Mediation Associates.

———. 1995. *Students Resolving Conflict: Peer Meditaron in Schools.* Glenview, IL: GoodYear Books.

Community Boards, and Ramón Alzate. 2000. *Transformación del Conflicto: Curriculum para Bachillerato y Secundaria.* Bilbao: Editorial Mensajero.

Cookson, Peter W. Jr., and Barbara Schneider, eds. 1995. *Transforming Schools.* New York: Garland.

Darling-Hammond, Linda. 1997. *The Right to Learn: A Blueprint for Creating Schools that Work.* San Francisco: Jossey-Bass.

DeVries, Rheta, and Betty Zan. 1994. *Moral Classrooms, Moral Children: Creating a Constructive Atmosphere in Early Education.* New York: Teachers College Press.

Faber, Adele, and Elaine Mazlish. 1996. *How to Talk so Kids Can Learn at Home and in School.* New York: Simon & Schuster.

Fernadez García, Isabel. 2001. *Guia para la convivencia en el aula.* Barcelona: CissPraxis.

Field, Harriet. 1996. "A Wholistic Approach to Conflict Resolution." Paper presented at the Association for Childhood Education International Study Conference, Minneapolis, April 10–13.

Hancock, Mary, Peter Gager, and Maurice J. Elias. 1993. *Factors Influencing the Effectiveness of Preventive and Social Competency Programs in New Jersey Public Schools*. New Brunswick, NJ: Rutgers University.

Jiménez Romero, Carlos. 2005. "Convivencia, conceptualización y sugerencias para la praxis." *Puntos de Vista: Cuadernos del Observatorio de las migraciones y la convivencia Intercultural de la Ciudad de Madrid* 1: 7–31.

Jones, Tricia S., Jennifer Batton, and W. L. Carruthers. 2000. "Conflict Resolution Education: Issues of Institutionalization." In *Does it Works? The Case for Conflict Resolution Education in our Nation's Schools*, edited by Tricia S. Jones and Daniel Kmitta. Washington D.C.: Conflict Resolution Education Network.

Jones, Tricia S., and Daniel Kmitta, eds. 2000. *Does it Work? The Case for Conflict Resolution Education in Our Nation's Schools*. Washington D.C.: Conflict Resolution Education Network.

Jones, Tricia S., Rebecca Sanford, and Andrea Bodtker. 2000. *The National Curriculum Integration Project: Report on Year One (1998–1999)*. Philadelphia: College of Allied Health Professions, Temple University.

Lederach, John Paul. 1984. *Educar para la paz. Objetivo escolar*. Barcelona, Fontamara. New edition in press under the title *ABC de la paz y los conflictos*. Madrid, Catarata.

Lorenzo, Manuel, and Antonio Bolívar, eds. 1997. *Trabajar en los márgenes. Asesoramiento, formación e innovación en contextos educativos problemáticos*. Granada: Instituto de Ciencias de la Educación.

Moreno, Juan Manuel, and Juan Carlos Torrego. 1999. *Resolución de conflictos de convivencia en centros escolares*. Colección de Educación Permanente. Madrid: UNED.

Noddings, Nel. 1992. *The Challenge to Care in Schools: An Alternative Approach to Education*. New York: Teachers College Press.

Olweus, Dan. 1993. *Bullying at School*. Oxford: Blackwell.

Ortega Ruiz, Rosario. 1998. *La convivencia escolar: qué es y cómo abordarla*. Sevilla: Consejería de Educación y Ciencia, Junta de Andalucía.

———. 2000. *Educar en la convivencia para prevenir la violencia.* Madrid: Colección Aprendizaje.

Proyecto Atlántida. 2003. *La convivencia democrática y la disciplina escolar.* Madrid: Proyecto Atlántida. At www.proyecto-atlantida.org/download/ConvivenciaLibro.pdf.

———. 2003. *Escuelas y familias democráticas.* Madrid: Proyecto Atlántida. At www.proyecto-atlantida.org/download/Escuelas%20y%20familiaLibro.pdf.

Sandy, Sandra V. 2001. "Conflict Resolution Education in the Schools: 'Getting There'." *Conflict Resolution Quarterly* 19, no. 2: 237–50.

Torrego, Juan Carlos. 1998. "Análisis de la problemática de convivencia y fases para la organización de la convivencia." *Organización y gestión educativa* 4: 19–31.

———. 2000. "La resolución de conflictos de convivencia en centros escolares. Una propuesta de formación del profesorado basada en el centro." Ph.D. Diss., UNED.

Trianes, Mª Victoria. 1996. *Educación y competencia social. Un programa en el aula.* Málaga: Ediciones Aljibe.

Part 2

Socioeducational Context in the Basque Country

6

Learning Communities: A Basque Egalitarian Educational Project

MAITE ARANDIA LOROÑO, ISABEL MARTÍNEZ DOMÍNGUEZ,
and IÑAKI SANTA CRUZ AYO

In this chapter we discuss the development process for the Learning Communities project in the Basque Country: its origins, its features, what steps
have been taken within this sociopolitical context for its implementation
in schools, what educational principles are shared, what types of innova-
tions are underway, as well as the types of work undertaken so far within
the existing school network. We will approach this process using as a reference, on the one hand, the bilingual nature of the community, and on the
other, the potential and strength of an educational model that not only is
underway at different stages (early childhood, primary, secondary, adult
education), but in various types of schools (public, private, and ikastolas[1]),
within different contexts (urban and rural), and with different types of
communities, for example, penitentiaries. In this particular setting, the
Basque Country is developing the first such experience.

Learning Communities is a global transformation project involving
school educational practices, with the expectation of overcoming inequities, providing excellence in education in order to achieve not only greater
competence within this knowledge society, but also contribute to social
cohesion. Inclusive egalitarian and dialogue-based education theories
and practices, which have demonstrated their efficiency and usefulness in
producing instrumental learning and improving social and educational

---

1. Schools where instruction is carried out exclusively in Basque.

interaction, are taken as benchmarks. The leveraged process of change is rooted in a series of key factors: the value of community and community-oriented education of individuals, inclusion of the social capital represented by family members and their training, the actual opening of schools to the community and its dynamics, the development of dialogue-based procedures within education and in the relational world inside the school.

The Basque Country is a pioneer in the implementation and development of this project. Beginning in 1996, first experimentally at four schools, through an agreement between the Basque government Department of Education and the CREA (the University of Barcelona's *Centre Especial de Recerca en Teories I Pràctiques Superadores de Desigualtats* (Center for Research in Theories and Practices for Overcoming Inequities]), and then since 2000, it has been powered by its own consulting team. This team has been nurturing the training of its agents, the experiential exchange between the schools in this community and others, and the development of innovative projects, assuring systematic progress in the process of change.

Along these fourteen years, the project has been strengthened and extended to a broad network of schools. These schools have introduced core changes to organizational structures, management processes, methodologies, and community relations; and this is making it possible to increase school success as well as to improve social interaction inside and outside the classrooms and schools.

Theoretical Foundations: Academic Bases and Background

Unfortunately, many policies and educational projects in our society have been based on obsolete theories, on erroneous interpretations of key authors, or on simple beliefs and ideas without any academic basis. However, improvement in education cannot begin from a basis of superstition. It must take as its genesis the most insightful and up to date societal analyses available. These should be supported by theories that provide not only descriptions, but also elements for transformation. The Learning Communities project is rooted in contributions from internationally recognized theory and research and educational practices that have produced better results by linking increased learning and social interaction (Elboj et al. 2002). The project has as its benchmark the analyses of the current information society, indicating that the key element conditioning the productivity of a country, a region, a business, and the individual is the ability to select and process information; this ability is very closely related to attained education levels. Consequently, in order to counteract duality and social exclusion, it is necessary to instill in all individuals the knowledge that will allow them access to the information society; learning must occupy a central place, particularly in those settings with greater risk of exclusion.

This idea is contradicted by the motto so often repeated in the Spanish state: "adapting to diversity." During the past twenty years, one of history's most prominent and transformational psychologists, Lev S. Vygotsky (1978, 1986), has been persistently associated with a constructivism involved in adaptations; this would doom to a slower pace and to a lesser amount of essential learning those with the least possibilities of learning. However, a reading of his works demonstrates that nowhere does the author address this focus on adaptation, but quite the contrary, the focus is on transforming the surroundings in order to achieve greater amounts of learning. Thus, Learning Communities uses as a theoretical basis a communicative concept of learning—*dialogue-based learning*—developed by José Ramón Flecha (1997) and Adriana Aubert and colleagues (2008).

Dialogue-based learning recognizes the major role of all interactions (not only teacher-student interactions) in the learning process and, consequently, emphasizes cooperation of the various educational agents (students, families, external agents, and professionals), while considering dialogue the source of all learning. The communicative concept of learning fits within the broader framework of dual theories in social sciences: from the point of view of the latter, reality is not the result of systems, or actions by individuals, but of the continued interaction between the two. On the other hand, dialogue occupies an increasingly central role in the relationships among individuals, and between individuals and institutions. This has been defined as a "dialogical spin" in current society by José Ramón Flecha, Jesús Gómez, and Lidia Puigvert (2001). From the standpoint of critical pedagogy, Paulo Freire (1969) through his theory of dialogue-based action had already formulated the dialogue-based nature of the human being and of its relation to the world. For Freire, dialogicity is not a methodological or technical issue, but a stance toward understanding and change, which implies confidence in its possibility. From the standpoint of philosophy, Jürgen Habermas twelve years later wrote the *Theory of Communicative Action* (1981), where he defends in all individuals the capabilities of language and action, and egalitarian dialogue based on claims of validity and not on claims of power, as a means for coordinating action. He addresses the insufficiency of a concept of rationality limited to a sole player oriented toward his own goals, and develops the idea of a communicative rationality, which assumes several subjects interacting, reaching an agreement. Other theoretical contributions, such as symbolic interactivism from George Mead (1934) or the universal language capability from Noam Chomsky (1988), agree on the role of intersubjectivity as a source of transformation at a social, educational, and personal level.

Dual and dialogue-based theories arise from the recognition of practices that already achieve understanding through dialogue. Research on successful educational efforts shows that the projects able to transform situations of failure and conflict into success and social interaction have developed strategies of participation, dialogue, and reaching agreements aimed at overcoming obstacles and inequities. Among the projects and practices, in the educational setting, that have attained and are achieving the greatest success in delivering quality learning, greater parity, mutual support, and social interaction, we will analyze three experiences: the La Verneda-Sant Martí Adult School (Sánchez 1999) and two international experiences: the School Development Program (Comer 1997) and the Accelerated Schools (Levin 1987).

La Verneda-Sant Martí Adult School

The Learning Communities project began at this school, which was created in 1978 by a group of people from the Sant-Martí district in Barcelona. This school is defined as a diverse, participatory, democratic educational center, self-contained in the neighborhood, free of charge, striving for equality in the cultural and educational fields of adult individuals. Certain transformational educational practices have been developed at this school; for example, literary social gatherings (*"tertulias literarias dialógicas"*; Flecha-García 1997) where individuals who have recently become literate and without academic levels, read and discuss universal literature classics such as Joyce's *Ulysses*, Kafka's "The Metamorphosis," and many others. The school's organization is based on everyone's participation through egalitarian dialogue in connection with learning, as well as in terms of organization and management. Another feature of the school is its involvement in transforming the neighborhood of La Verneda, as a founding member and participating since its inception.

School Development Program

This project began in 1968 with the demands of an African-American community in New Haven, Connecticut concerned about the low achievement rates and serious confrontations taking place at some schools. The project was originally intended for two area schools on behalf of the Child Study Center at Yale University, under the direction of James Comer. The program was able to accomplish drastic reforms in those schools, and has since expanded to hundreds of schools. The philosophy of this program is explained by the African proverb: "It takes a village to raise a child." Therefore, it involves the mobilization of all individuals and communities related to the school, in order to achieve student success in all aspects: academic, personal, and social. The program is guided by three basic principles: collaboration from all individuals, decision-making by consensus, and no-fault problem solving. An organizational change is proposed at the school, based on creating three teams; of these, the school planning and management team is the most important, consisting of representatives from management, faculty, students, and families. It is responsible for providing a sense of direction to the school, prioritizing and coordinating activities, and making sure that no one assumes ownership of the program and its results.

Accelerated Schools

This is a program initiated in 1986 by Henry Levin, at that time a professor at Stanford University. The project has subsequently grown and currently involves more than one thousand schools. One of the goals is planning the studies for all students at a maximum potential, so that no student falls behind for purposes of secondary or higher education. It involves accelerating the learning process and increasing the expectations for success, while applying in disadvantaged schools strategies used in the learning process of high-achieving students. As a result, schools that were among the lowest rated in standardized tests are now above the median. Also, for this project to succeed the involvement of all communities is essential: faculty, students, nonteaching staff, relatives, volunteers, and environmental factors.

Learning Communities takes into consideration and adopts, from the outset, these theoretical-practical benchmarks that serve as basis to develop its own approach to the educational transformation processes at schools in the Basque Country, and currently in many other areas of the Spanish state and elsewhere in the world.

The Learning Communities Project in the Basque Country: Origins and Direction

The history of the Learning Communities project in the Basque Country goes back to the 1990s, when the Ruperto Medina Elementary School, located in a neighborhood of Portugalete along the left margin of the Bilbao estuary, learned during the 1980s about Henry Levin's "Accelerated Schools" project. The school was seeking an educational plan that would help overcome the learning difficulties its students were facing. Initial steps were taken in that direction and then, with some trepidation, the entire faculty and parents involved with the school decided to become the first Learning Community in the Basque Country. With this initiative as starting point, and with a positive assessment of the new possibilities this type of project, the Basque government's Department of Education entered into a four-year agreement with the University of Barcelona's CREA educational research center. The Learning Communities began as an experimental project to implement transformation in at-risk schools in the three territories of Bizkaia, Araba, and Gipuzkoa. Four schools were selected, under CREA's mentorship, and at the same time the structure was developed for the Basque Country's own team to follow-up, facilitate, and mentor the project. Importantly, the leading actors in the implementation and development of that experimental project at the schools were the faculty and staff, students, and families, in addition to individual consultants and volunteers, who actively participated for its success. Also relevant is the fact that the Basque Country is an autonomous community with two official languages: the Basque language Euskara, and Spanish. The two languages vary in use and fluency depending on territory and towns. One major goal in this project is to make it possible for the students to have the linguistic skills required in both languages. During the first four years an internal and external assessment process was undertaken to observe the student and school progress, as well as overall context. The assessment verified improved results in the students' learning processes; therefore, given the noticeable educational impact the Basque government decided to institutionally promote, starting with the 2000–01 academic year, the Learning Communities project, with a strong commitment toward implementation in the schools involved in the experimental phase, and extending it to other schools in the Basque Country. To achieve this purpose, on the one hand, a support structure was developed consisting of educational consultants from nearby each school, and a person serving as general coordinator for the project, which also has support from University of the Basque Country. At the same time, and within the general plan for nonuniversity teacher training, a specific training course was developed with the purpose of making this project known to interested schools. One of the selection criteria for participating in the course was to have in attendance more than one person per school, thus facilitating the task of reflecting on the challenges information society creates for the educational system as a whole, and to the transformative work at each particular school to develop a Learning Community. As a consequence of this first academic year, three more Bizkaian schools, with management teams that had taken part in the training, requested support to initiate the "awareness stage," and made the decision to join the four schools already in the project.

In view of the project's success, since 2004 the Basque government's Department of Education has called for bids in connection with innovation projects specific to the Learning Communities. In 2007, this project was included as part of the priority guidelines for educational innovation.[2] In the bid proposal for the term 2007–10, supported by the assessment of results attained in the preceding three-year period, the program was included within the *"Eje 2. Una escuela mejor"*/*"2. Ardatza. Eskola hobea"* ("Core Item 2. A Better School,") under the heading *"Calidad de aprendizaje: éxito escolar para todos y todas"*/*"Ikaskuntzaren kalitatea: Arrakasta guztientzat"* ("Quality in Learning: Academic Success for Everyone"). Thus, on the basis of the approaches developed by the international scientific community in connection with dialogue-based learning (Flecha-García and Lerena 2008; Flecha-García 1997; Jaussi 2002; Elboj et al. 2002; Feito and López 2008; Freire 1969, 1973, 1995; Aubert et al. 2008; Alcalde 2006); the following goals are proposed for the Comunidad Autónoma del País Vasco/Euskal Autonomia Erkidegoa (CAPV/EAE, Autonomous Community of the Basque Country): Design school transformation processes in harmony with the transformation from industrial to information society; implement processes for training and experimentation from the standpoint of dialogue-based learning; develop strategies to leverage interactions related to learning in the classroom, at the school, and in the community at large; develop the community-based model for conflict prevention; and, finally, promote community involvement in all educational processes.

---

2. See: www.hezkuntza.ejgv.euskadi.net (last accesed January 21, 2010).

The Department of Education's commitment to the project reached its pinnacle in 2008 when a macro-conference on Learning Communities (*Ikaskom*) was organized. With the motto "quality for all students," the intent is for this showcase to introduce, on the one hand, the project and practices developed by the various schools in the Learning Communities network; and on the other hand, to disseminate the Basque government's expansion and implementation plan.

Having reviewed the project for almost fifteen years in our autonomous community, we can affirm its successful implementation and dissemination to new schools and educational levels. As of early 2010, twenty-eight schools (seventeen in Bizkaia, six in Araba, and five in Gipuzkoa) are at various stages of Learning Community initiation and development. Four other schools are in the initial "awareness" phase: three in Bizkaia and one in Gipuzkoa. These are primary (ages six to twelve), secondary (ages twelve to eighteen), and adult education schools. In this latter case, it is worth mentioning that in 2009 the training classroom at a penitentiary located in Araba joined the project. This has produced great expectations for the project's expansion and its transformative potential in communities traditionally excluded from an egalitarian education.

Stages and Phases in the Process of Transforming Schools into Learning Communities

The transformation of a school into a Learning Community is addressed as a systematic process in various stages and phases, which in each case should be contextualized, debated, and agreed upon by the school's entire educational community. In the case of the Basque Country project, each school has the autonomy to decide on the sequence or the timing of their journey through these stages and phases, provided that the school stays true to the principles that guide this project, and that, integratively, we can distill into a single condition: the participatory dialogue of all of the community's individuals. Thus, while the initial schools completed each phase step by step, those who joined later, drawing on their predecessor's learning processes, have developed several phases simultaneously.

The transformation process is divided into two periods: a stage prior to the school's joining the project during which the entire educational community learns about and commits to the project (the "awareness" and "decision-making" phases); and project development and integration, which involves the school's continuing the process and transforming into a Learning Community. This includes the phases of "dream," "priority selection," "planning," "project implementation," "research," "training," and "assessment."

Awareness Phase

The goal of this phase is for the entire school community to become acquainted with the transformation project and to analyze the situation from its core and context. For this purpose, brainstorming sessions take place involving everyone in the community, dealing with the following topics: principles of a learning community, the process of school transformation, information society educational challenges, the new forms of social and educational inequality this entails, and successful models and practices to overcome school failure. Needs are also analyzed, as well as the school and community's strong and weak points. Conclusions reached are discussed and made known to all members of the educational community.

Decision-making Phase

Here the entire education community commits to the transformation process and decides to join the project.

Dream Phase

The true process of school transformation begins with the dream. The entire education community visualizes the school desired, setting aside limiting factors; gathers all inputs needed for change; agrees as to the focus of efforts, and contextualizes the Learning Communities' basic principles at the particular school.

Priority Selection Phase

In this phase a contrast is made between reality and dream, in order to find out which aspects of that reality should be changed, and their order of priority. This involves an in-depth quantitative and qualitative analysis of the school and community's reality. Beginning from this reflection, members identify what to eliminate, leverage, and transform in order create the "dream" school, and prioritize transformative process efforts.

Planning Phase

In this phase, each priority's action plan is designed. It constitutes the first instance of community participation in the decision-making process regarding curricular and organizational matters that will guide the school's day-to-day work. Structures must be created that facilitate encounters between members and promote critical thinking on the strategies for change. Different working groups are set up in order to prepare initiatives and deliverables for each priority. Depending on the task assigned, these groups consist of faculty, families, students, volunteers, members of local associations, and advisers. On the basis of their proposals, the management team, the faculty and staff, the school council and the parents association make the decisions on what plans of action to carry out.

Project Implementation Phase

This phase begins with the implementation of the steps planned in connection with each priority. Thus, a process of innovation and experimentation begins, where progress is made toward solidifying the project, by means of analysis, assessment, and critical thinking in terms of the changes introduced.

Research, Training, and Assessment Phases

Research, understood as critical thinking on action; training community members in terms of the process requirements; and continuous assessment are inseparable elements that are present throughout the entire process of transforming a school into a Learning Community.

Common Practices between Learning Communities Schools

Each school's project decisions differ depending on particular priorities. However, there are a series of common practices that arise from shared values, and from the debate and joint critical thinking they have been engaged in. The include joint committees, learning contracts, dialogue-based social gatherings, interactive groups, and the training of professionals, family members and volunteers.

Joint Committees

These working groups consist of family members, professionals, students, and other social and educational agents. They play a leading role in project development, implementation, and assessment. Their number and nature, be it stable or temporary, will depend in each school on specific issues and priorities. Their work uses as starting point proposals set forth on the basis of egalitarian dialogue in which each individual contributes his/her views and arguments.

Learning Contract

This is a document that contains, as a minimum, teacher, student, and family commitments to each child's learning process. All contents must be developed, agreed upon, and accepted by all the individuals signing the contract. It is part of each student's profile, intended to create high expectations on what can be learned, and serves as framework for the constant assessment of each student's path, as well as pertinent changes to be introduced regarding progress. It may adopt different forms at each school.

Dialogue-based Social Gatherings

This is a communications strategy aimed at the collective construction of knowledge (Alonso Olea, Arandia, and Loza 2008; Arandia, Alonso-Olea, and Martínez-Domínguez 2010). It involves agreeing to read a text in common, and participants individually select and present a particular paragraph they wish to share with the rest of the group, because that paragraph has drawn their attention or evokes certain memories. An egalitarian dialogue is established, in which arguments take precedence, regardless of the power ranking within the group of the person presenting those arguments. Although the structure follows along the lines of a literary roundtable, these social gatherings are not limited exclusively to literary texts, but extend to other types of texts and documents, for example, from different disciplinary areas, or with strictly pedagogical content, and so on. They may also include other formats and languages, such as music and cinema, depending on the social gathering's goals. Thus, they become a powerful training tool that is used in the training of professionals, students, volunteers, and family members, and in various physical settings (classrooms, library, meeting rooms). In all cases, egalitarian and democratic participation is facilitated for all individuals in the education community, on various topics under debate at the school, regardless of their membership in a group of professionals, parents, or other participant agents, or of the contents' greater or lesser level of specialization.

Interactive Groups

This is a methodological strategy that comes from dialogue-based learning. It involves the participation of several adults in the classroom, in coordination with a professional responsible for the group, and starting with heterogeneous clusters they promote interactions between peers, as well as between these individuals and the students. In these groups, the more varied their constituency, the more abundant will the resulting interactions be, with greater possibilities for learning, and for a resulting dynamic whereby all participants feel responsible for their own learning process and that of others.

Training of Professionals, Family Members, and Volunteers

The process of transforming a school into a Learning Community inevitably becomes an incentive for the training of all members of that community, besides the students. Dialogue-based learning serves also as frame of reference, and is understood as a process aimed at having a bearing on personal, professional, institutional, and social changes in each school's context. To conclude this section, we will add that in the case of the Basque Country, we have significant examples of the impact of the transformation of its schools into Learning Communities, which make it possible to visualize that its dream can come true. In this regard, six students from the Sansomendi[3] lecture room building in the Miguel de Unamuno secondary school in Vitoria-Gasteiz (Araba), a Learning Community established in 2007 at a school with a high failure rate, received in January 2010 the prize for the best interview as part of the contest in *Correo Digital*, the online version of a major newspaper in the Basque Country. The other three winning teams were from two private schools and a public one with a high success rate.

Project Sustainability Factors

The profound nature of the change entailed in the Learning Communities project is a process of reclaiming the meaning of education as a basic right and as a process for empowering all individuals. We know that profound changes are difficult. They require a fresh approach in terms of educational, relational, and organizational structures; solid support must be provided to those individuals who undertake them, thus making it possible to address the complexity of the challenges; and they must guarantee consistency within the project. Maintaining this consistency, moreover, requires the delivery of something beyond words.

---

3. See www.elcorreo.com/alava/20100113/mas-actualidad/sociedad/instituto-miguel-unamuno-vitoria-201001131657.html.

In specific terms, this requires: *Continual awareness* of the scope of the educational transformation, resulting in a community that learns by means of dialogue and social interaction. *Trusting people*, sustaining high expectations for their learning potential and their ability to contribute to the project. *Introducing methodologies* that encourage social interaction, commitment to learning, and dialogue-based relationships. *Incorporating new technologies*, treating them as windows open to the world and to the possibility for producing divergent knowledge. Within participating schools, *creating an atmosphere rooted in deliberative democracy and participatory action*. In this atmosphere, the community as a whole behaves as an authentic historical subject and protagonist in education. Finally, there must be *institutional support* for the creation of organizational structures that facilitate and provide continuous counsel to participating schools. All of these factors are essential for maintaining the project as a whole over time.

The project is relatively simple in terms of phases and strategies. Its complexity, however, resides in the internal process created for the purpose of working methodically and systematically, aiming for an in-depth analysis of each step that the schools and their dynamics keep generating. The ultimate purposes of this rigorous method of proceeding are: to generate greater technical-practical knowledge of the overall process of educational transformation; gather evidence on the impact that change generates in the learning process of the community and of the different agents that make up the community; and verify the inclusionary effect of the social context of each school. Next, we will describe the various elements that have ensured the sustainability of the project. To describe this, we will refer to two major parameters.

The *educational* parameter refers to educational, formative, and innovative research, and dissemination plans and actions to guarantee academically based educational programs and consequent excellence in learning. In the *organizational* parameter, external structures have been extended to provide support and counseling to the project and for the needs (personal, community, formative, and organizational) arising from its implementation and development; as well as internal structures developed at schools to guarantee the inclusion of all voices in the learning community's decision-making processes. The educational parameter addresses training, research, and socialization of knowledge, while the organizational parameter includes external and dialogue-based organizational structures.

Training: A Method for Change to Take Root

Permanent education is not merely a discursive idea, but an idea in action that shows us the opportunity we have for continuous learning, provided we are open to it. This must be intentially planned in a school. Thus, continual training is an essential element for the Learning Communities project. At first, it develops a sense of transformation and instills the conceptual and procedural tools that can be utilized. As the project matures, continuing education of all participants ensures critical thinking and advancement in Learning Communities core subject areas; it also provides for the inclusion of new issues arising from the energy and dynamics of a living project; finally, it provides a sense of project ownership in all actors.

Schools customarily think of continuing training as oriented toward teachers. However, in this case it is aimed at all individuals involved with different levels of dedication and responsibility to the project. It responds to a yearly plan crafted on the contents and training modality to be employed, and can take place in homogeneous (each community separately) or mixed clusters.

Given that the project is sustained on the conviction that knowledge is something we build jointly, and that knowledge is a direct consequence of social interaction between the various actors, it is important to select a training model that is not merely a transmitter. Every training process must be geared toward creating spaces that are authentic places for critical thinking, studying, debating, producing knowledge, and projecting transformative actions. Methodological strategies such as dialogue-based social gatherings and interactive groups better support this type of process. Among the numerous developed training processes, we should point out "awareness" training as a step prior to the decision to initiate the process of educational transformation.

Awareness training is an important step toward educational expansion and restructuring; it has a two-fold objective: First, it shares project tools and on-the-ground knowledge for developing the project in schools. The goal is not to retread well-trodden paths, but to make knowledge available to the Learning Communities network about encountered problems; improvement of methodological tools; family, volunteer, and social agent inclusion; introduction of diversity into the school's everyday life;

and other relevant project matters. Second, it performs a thorough diagnosis of the schools that wish to become involved, unveiling, on the one
hand, their potentials for developing a relational atmosphere, their internal atmospheres, the status of families and external actors, and greater
or lesser clarity on the decision-making process regarding change; it also
allows for the detection of weak points that should be priority items when
addressing the project.

Researching Innovative Thematic Projects: Theorization as a Key to Evolution

Annually, each community school puts forward one or several central
topics involving their study and educational work, and data is gathered
and analyzed on these topics in connection with their day-to-day implementation. This inquisitive spirit makes it possible to analyze in greater
depth the educational strategies applied and the project's educational
impact on the community and to improve methods employed. A record of
the greater or lesser academic success attained by the students should also
be kept. This procedural method has led to theorization on educational
topics including information society, dialogue-based learning, dialogue-
based practices, interactive groups, training of and participation by family
members, models for social interaction, learning contracts, multilingual
approaches, and skills and their assessment. The project can also be enriched through the production of living documents that are made available
to the social and academic community.[4]

Immediate Sharing of Knowledge

One established principle of the project is to share the knowledge gathered with the network of schools in terms of methodological procedures,
utilized resources, encountered problems, and major steps to be taken;
as well as to check contrasting evidence on the overall educational value.
The habit of systematically sharing theoretical issues in connection with
all ongoing projects, makes it possible for other Learning Communitiesy
to avoid retracing steps and paths already taken by others, and to begin at
the point where others have ended their analysis. A detailed written description of the educational processes performed (who particpated, how it

---

4. Learning Communities, www.utopiadream.info/red/tiki-index.php.

was done, what results it produced, and what was learned, together with any other relevant information) should be produced, debated, and analyzed within each school. It should consider shared and different elements, as well as necessary changes. New theoretical and practical elements arising from internal school debates are incorporated in the final document. This document serves as a record of the project's status with regards to a particular issue and is the starting point for processes that other network schools may wish to initiate.

Therefore, this document serves four purposes: it is a benchmark for any school that wishes to explicitly address that particular issue, it is a working document for new schools, it serves to raise awareness in schools, and it is a workguide for teacher, administrator, volunteer, and family training. This allows the subject matter to be contextualized, adapted, and readdressed at other schools.

External Organizational Structures: A Method for Supporting and Advising

For a project of this nature to stay on track and grow, it requires not only internal research momentum, but also external organizational structures to advise about and share the experience. In the Basque Country we have various structures at our disposal: A stable structure, consisting of the project coordinators from each school involved, advisors from each region where a school is located, a lead person in charge from the university, and a general project coordinator. They support the specific projects of every school for each academic year, promote training, hold meetings to discuss and learn from each school's proposals, and provide theoretical insight. This latter occurs during dialogue-based social gatherings at which educational texts are presented that lead to critical thinking on active projects. Monthly meetings take place for purposes of this followup. There is also a network of Learning Communities, each with a philosophy of sharing and socialization of accumulated knowledge. Their intention is to reveal and share theoretical and practical inputs that can be incorporated at other schools.

Dialogue-based School Organizational Structures

New organizations in each school have a very powerful educational and cohesive effect. These include joint committees set up around the school's priority needs that involve teachers, students, families, volunteers, and social agents; and delegates' assemblies, which are elected in each classroom, that represent students and even their families.

The creation of these structures, as well as the type of work strategies they utilize, serve to facilitate new methods of understanding educational participation. This produces a true sense of individual belonging in a project. In this regard, joint committees guarantee a level playing field in the school's curricular and organizational decision-making processes. In these committees the voices of students, family members, volunteers, teachers, nonteaching staff, and other social agents are and feel equally important. This way of addressing educational priorities that are deemed valuable highlights in an experiential way new methods of internalizing the logic of participating in the social and educational world. The impact resulting from the work this structure generates is crucial, due above all to the feeling of actually being a real and valuable participant in the school's and the community's dynamics. In turn, the delegates' assemblies, with delegates selected from among students as well as among family members, facilitate educational debate in classrooms, and share generated ideas. This provides much greater meaning to the focused work developed by the joint committee, and establishes fluid communicative dynamics at the school.

Conclusion

In this chapter, we have examined how drastic change in the educational reality of schools can and actually is taking place. The general values of this process are diversity, a level playing field, and inclusiveness. Making these features a reality in the schools involved in the Learning Communities project in the Basque Country is having major effects on the participating individuals, schools, and communities.

Each project is and should be rooted on a solid theoretical foundation endorsed by research and academic literature regarding efficient and useful educational practices for improving social and school interaction. Its main goals are to achieve excellence in education for everyone and to facilitate social cohesion. Progress toward these goals is being met through the actual and visible opening of schools to the community and its dynamics, and also by including in the life of each school all stakeholders: family members, volunteers, and other community members.

The end results are geared toward wholescale change at the school and its surroundings. Its positive results are being compiled in the world of relationships between the various actors and in the positive interaction at school, within the family, and in the social context. It begins with the assumption that the school belongs to everyone and must work to achieve social inclusion. This concept results in the participation of the various educational actors in all the related decision-making processes: educational, organizational, and social. In each school this is facilitating the process of cohesion between different cultures and communities, unity, and interaction between different generations.

The root of the Learning Community is a dialogue-based and community-oriented educational outlook, which is materialized in a school's democratic organization. This has a major impact in terms of increased participation and broad agreements and shared responsibilities by all members of the school community.

It is based on a perception that deems egalitarian dialogue as a source of learning. This concept leads to the integration of other actors into the educational task with the students, such as: family members, volunteers, or other educational or social agents. The inclusion of these varied relationships is producing an impact, not only in terms of improved learning results for students, but also improved family interactions, and improved relations between faculty and students, and professionals and families, as long as there is a recognition of the value of "the other." Dialogue-based methodology, such as social gatherings and interactive groups, has a proven effectiveness in improving school performance.

Learning Communities projects follow a rigorous research-action process that makes it possible to train every participant and structure a solidly based theorization on educational practices to achieve academic success and improve social interaction both inside and outside the classrooms and participating schools.

In conclusion, we wish to emphasize not only the value of dreams and utopia, as Freire stated, but also the importance of educational comprehensiveness. These are both essential elements in this project of social and educational transformation. It is a permanent search for answers and actions aimed at promoting a Basque society with real presence in the world. Pointing in that direction requires an understanding of the educational and social actions within a broader perspective of democratizing social and educational settings, and steps that actively include the community in the analysis and exploration of different paths for today's educational issues. The Learning Communities project, currently underway with a tremendous joint effort, contributes to that goal. It responds to the goal of making sure education reaches all individuals, facilitates overcoming origin-based inequities, in addition to making it possible for the Basque Country to become an educational benchmark of excellence in the current academic and political landscape.

References

Alonso-Olea, Maria José, Maite Arandia, and Miguel Loza. 2008. "La tertulia como estrategia metodológica en la formación continua: avanzando en las dinámicas dialógicas." *REIFOP* 11, no. 1. April 10. www.aufop.com/aufop/home/.

Alcalde, Ana Isabel, ed. 2006. *Transformando la escuela. Las comunidades de aprendizaje.* Caracas: Editorial Laboratorio Educativo.

Arandia, Maite, Maria José Alonso-Olea, and Isabel Martínez-Domínguez. 2010. "La metodología dialógica en las aulas universitarias." *Revista de Educación* 351 (April): 75–95.

Aubert, Adriana, Ainhoa Flecha, Carme García, Ramón Flecha, and Sandra Racionero. 2008. *Aprendizaje dialógico en la sociedad de la información.* Barcelona: Hipatia.

Chomsky, Noam. 1988. *Language, Minds and Politics.* New York: Black Rose Books.

Comer, James. 1997. *Waiting for a Miracle: Why Schools Can't Solve Our Problems and How We Can.* New York: Dutton.

Comunidades de aprendizaje. At www.utopiadream.info/red/tiki-index.php.

Elboj, Carmen, Ignasi Puigdellivol, Marta Soler, and Rosa Valls. 2002. *Comunidades de Aprendizaje. Transformar la educación.* Barcelona: Graó.

Feito, Rafael, and Juan Ignacio López. 2008. *Construyendo escuelas democráticas.* Barcelona: Hipatia.

Flecha-García, Jose Ramón. 1997. *Compartiendo palabras. El aprendizaje de las personas adultas a través del diálogo.* Barcelona: Paidos.

Flecha-García, Jose Ramón, Jesús Gómez, and Lidia Puigvert. 2001. *Teoría sociológica contemporánea.* Barcelona: Paidós.

Flecha-García, José Ramón, and Rosa Lerena. 2008. *Comunidades de aprendizaje.* Sevilla: Fundación ECOEM.

Freire, Paulo. 1969. *Pedagogy of the Oppressed.* Translated by Myra Berg-man Ramos. Cambridge, MA: Harvard University Press.

———. 1973. *Education for Critical Consciousness.* New York: Seabury Press.

———. 1995. *A sombra desta mangueira.* Sao Paulo: Olho d'agua. Eng-lish-language version: *Pedagogy of the Heart,* 1997, notes by Ana Maria Araújo Freire, translated by Donaldo Macedo and Alexandre Oliveira, foreword by Martin Carnoy, preface by Ladislau Dowbor. New York: Continuum.

Habermas, Jürgen. 1981. *Theorie des kommunikativen Handelns. Band I. Handlungsrationalität und gesellschaftliche Rationalisierung,.* Vol. 1. Frankfurt: Suhrkamp Verlag, 1981.

———. 1981. *Theorie des kommunikativen Handlens. Band II. Zur Kritik der funktionalistischen Vernunft.* Vol. 2. Frankfurt: Suhrkamp Ver-lag, 1981. English-language translation: *The Theory of Communica-tive Action,* 1984, translated by Thomas McCarthy. 2 vols. Boston: Beacon Press.

Jaussi, Maria Luisa, ed. 2002. *Comunidades de Aprendizaje en Euskadi/ Euskadiko Ikaskuntza Komunitateak.* Vitoria-Gasteiz: Servicio Cen-tral de Publicaciones del Gobierno Vasco.

Levin, Henry. 1987. "New Schools for the Disadvantaged." *Teacher Edu-cation Quartely* 14, no 4: 60–83.

Mead, George Herbert. *Mind, Self and Society from the Standpoint of a Social Behaviorist.* Chicago: the University of Chicago Press, 1934.

Sánchez, Montserrat. "La Verneda-Sant Marti: A School Where People Dare to Dream." *Harvard Educational Review* 69, no. 3 (1999): 320–35.

Vygotsky, Lev. 1978. *Mind in Society: Development of Higher Psychologi-cal Processes.* Edited by Michael Cole et al. Cambridge MA: Harvard University Press.

———. 1986. *Thought and Language.* Translation newly revised and edited by Alex Kozulin. Cambridge, MA: MIT Press.

7

Migrants en Route: Community Socioeducational Action

MIKEL ARRIAGA LANDETA and BEGOÑA ABAD MIGUÉLEZ

Situation of Migrant Children and Youth in the Basque Country

Data available confirm the ongoing growth of the immigrant population in the Basque Country.[1] But particularly the data confirm a growing number of immigrant youth or adolescents,[2] including second generation—those born in the Basque Country—as well as those arriving due to family regrouping, and even those arriving alone.

These youth represent new populations that must integrate into the institutions in their country of residence, and among these institutions the school system occupies a prominent place.[3] At school, by means of the

---

1. Based on data gathered by the Spanish National Institute of Statistics (Instituto Nacional de Estadística) (INE), in 1999 there were 16,793 foreigners residing in the Basque Country. In 2008 this figure reached 117,337.

2. According to data from the INE, in 1999 there were 6,291 foreign youth, ages zero through twenty-nine, residing in the Basque Country. In 2008 their numbers reached 56,068.

3. According to the Spanish Ministry of Education, there were 1,766 foreign students enrolled in schools in the Comunidad Autónoma del País Vasco/Euskal Autonomia Erkidegoa (CAPV/EAE, Autonomous Community of the Basque Country) for academic year 1998–99; this figure was 21,385 for academic year 2008–9. In terms of distribution by levels, we notice that all have shown a noticeable increase in enrollment by this type of students, although it is true that the largest contingent is reflected at the compulsory education levels. Thus, in Childhood Education, foreign students at CAPV/EAE schools increased from 33 during 1999–2000 to 3,613 during the academic year 2008–9; in elementary education, foreign students increased from 921 to 7,749 during the same period; in secondary education, foreign students at CAPV/EAE schools numbered 575 in 1999–2000, and rose to 5,280 in the 2008–9 academic year. Finally, in

instruction they receive as well as through the relationships they establish, these youth begin the process of acquiring knowledge and the lifestyle of the host society: language, beliefs, and customs. They also become familiar with the experience of being different, and with the level of acceptance or rejection this generates. Finally, they are able to obtain the intellectual and professional training that will allow them some day to occupy a job and a position within the social structure. Thus, the relevance of school in the process of solving the challenge of societal co-inclusion between natives and immigrants is indisputable (Abad Miguélez 2009).

The Basque educational system has undertaken reforms oriented toward this goal. The Special Educational Plan approved by the Basque Government in 1982 established integration of schools as one of its tenets; this acquired judicial status by means of Basque Public School Law 1/1993. It affirms that "public powers guarantee the provision of free and quality instruction for all, in a bilingual, diverse, Basque public school, serving Basque society, socially and culturally rooted in its environment, participatory, compensating for inequalities, and integrating diversity." Decree 118/1998 ordered an educational response to develop a comprehensive and integrated school for students with special educational needs—including underprivileged social or cultural situations—and assigning resources for educational intervention directed at students with serious adaptation difficulties.

The *measures for addressing diversity issues* that are gradually being developed include *measures of a regular nature*, applicable on the basis of a coordinated scheduling that specifies measures such as flexible grouping in core areas, individual work under supervision, the participation of two instructors in the classroom, and the creation of support groups outside of regular school hours. Meanwhile, *extraordinary measures* are taken after the preceding regular measures fail. These measures seek to keep students from leaving school without the basic credentials, risking vulnerability and social exclusion.

Specific programs aimed at immigrant students are added to the above-mentioned measures applicable to all students. The *Program for Serving Immigrant Students* (2003) contains guidelines for schooling, acceptance, and responding to their linguistic, curricular, and tutorial

post secondary and vocational schools a noticeably smaller increase took place: from 175 post secondary students in 1999–2000 to 926 in 2008–9; and from 79 students enrolled in vocational school in 1999–2000 to 1,410 in the academic year 2008–9.

educational needs, as well as curriculum enrichment through the new student's specific cultural contribution. There is also faculty available for linguistic reinforcement in order to support learning the Basque language, Euskara, so that its knowledge becomes a factor for inclusion rather than exclusion.

Nevertheless, the question arises whether these measures—all somehow limited to the pedagogical relationship—are sufficient for purposes of addressing all the needs and elements that govern the process of integrating immigrant students. Various studies (Marchesi 2006; Calero 2006) show that educational results are influenced to a much greater extent by what happens outside of school than by what happens inside. Likewise, the school's operations depend much more on social inputs than on organizational models and educational practices.

These findings suggest a new generation of (not strictly or exclusively school-oriented) educational practices and policies that, in addition to matching the social inputs at the schools that support conditions of greater adversity, can affect the lives of the students not only inside and during school hours, but also in the local, community, and family setting in which they interact.

From Institutional Program to Educational Project

The increased multiculturalism of globablization has revived political and academic debate about social integration. The main focus in this debate has centered on the notorious inability of modern institutions when it comes to addressing a new reality and, therefore, the need to seek new players capable of acting efficiently. This reexamination, which in the sociopolitical arena has involved accepting weakness on the part of the traditional players—labor markets and unions—in favor of local actors and agreements (Lapeyronnie 1992), is evident in the debate on integrating students from disadvantaged sectors and/or immigrant origins. Here the struggle against scholastic failure and promotion of integration become two basic tasks entrusted to the local setting (Henriot-Van Zanten 1994, 72).[4]

---

4. One example of this type of policy focused on local matters is the Educational Priority Area, developed in France and Great Britain. In response to a positive discrimination policy in sensitive neighborhoods with high rates of school failure, this type of project sought intervention at the local level (neighborhood) as an all-encompassing educational sphere for children and adolescents at risk of exclusion. The project consisted of combining interventions at different levels (housing, employment, safety, instruction) and eliciting the cooperation of all stakehold-

The growing interest in the microsociological focus centered on local matters is just one form of expressing a shift from strictly pedagogical interaction toward the *educational sphere*—comprised, in a global sense, by all socialization spaces and students' ways of lives—and in a horizontal sense by other actors and socialization agents. This shift in interest cannot be explained solely by the specific educational needs required by the new students. This is the goal of what is known as what are known as the *compensatory measures*.[5] However, without denying the progress these policies may have implied in the fight for integration, the fact is that they remain within the framework of the pedagogical relationship (classrooms and/or supportive teachers, curricular diversification, and so on) without going beyond it in any case.

Understanding the above-mentioned shift in the focus of interest requires a critical approach with a greater range that addresses a wide-ranging transformation of the traditional school form. In our opinion, this need for transformation arises from the crisis in the *institutional program* that was the basis of the school form during modernity, and the gradual emergence of the *educational project* as an alternative idea.

From the Institutional Program . . .

The educational program of modernity was based on the development of a socialization process tending toward the uniformity and homogeneity of a national culture as the guarantor of stability and a safeguard of social order.

To put this program into practice, modernity was provided with an ad hoc school mechanism. This mechanism is what Françoise Dubet (2003) calls the "institutional program." This program defined the school on the basis of its main function: overcoming local constraints and determinisms in order to instill new generations with universal and transcendental

---

ers, from parents to teachers and including associative movements and the local administration itself. The intended result was to be able to shift from a project centered on neighborhood mobilization in favor of the school, to a project where the school would become the academic dimension of a broader device for handling sensitive neighborhoods.

5. Compensatory policies have a long history, beginning with the *affirmative action* policy established in the United States during the 1960s under the Kennedy and Johnson administrations. The goal of this policy was to offer equal access to social and political institutions to those groups that until then had been relatively excluded from the process. The aim was to carry out an early educational intervention designed to fight against sociocultural disadvantages. But the results did not meet expectations.

principles to form a broader and more homogeneous cultural framework, such that culture, society, and national (nation-state) territory would all come together as one.

This socialization task acquired the overtones of a sacred task because, after all, it was a matter of fostering in the "national citizenry" a sense of social responsibility in the "civil religion." In this sense, the sacred nature of the task implied the concept of the school as sanctuary; this place becomes closed within itself and is isolated from the chaos, in other words, human and mundane interests and passions. As in traditional religious orders, within the classroom the contents and disciplines are governed by an inherent logic, an academic logic that cross-references itself: parents are invited to relinquish the rights to teach their children to an institution, and families avoid participating in the institution's life and internal logic. This maintains a strict separation between society and school and strengthens the pedagogical fiction that schools address students as subjects for information, knowledge, and reasoning purposes, and not as the unique children and adolescents they are. The institutional program gives rise to a bureaucratic educational system that colonizes the living world of individuals and communities through the definition of what it deems legitimate knowledge (transmitted in the traditional setting and form of schooling) and a pedadogical relationship based on a hierarchically defined roles structure (Flecha 2009, 327).

. . . To the Educational Project

Françoise Dubet points out that "although school has been a modern institutional program, this does not make it less of an institutional program. Now that we are 'even more modern,' the contradictions of that program appear blatantly, not only under the effect of an outside threat, but also through an endogenous thrust in keeping with the actual seedlings of modernity" (2003, 229).

Prominent among these seedlings, because of its effects, is the breakdown of the culturally homogeneous national citizenry model. This is because political-symbolic and population movements—migrations but also movements of unrecognized or disadvantaged minorities, or supranational integration processes—increase "the polyethnicity of national populations or the multinationality of states" (Terrén 2003, 263).

Thus, the national narrative is no longer as solid and homogeneous, since today's citizen lives within a multitude of cultures and systems of reference beyond strictly national ones. Belongings have multiplied, and consequently creating sense depends on local constructions of values and social and political agreements. Therefore, it is no longer possible to assert the continuity between socialization and subjectivation. The uniqueness of individuals is now the cornerstone of the school form, where the student yields space in favor of children and adolescents as active subjects who must participate in their own education, commit to learning, develop their own projects, and express themselves.

It could be said that the climate of weariness and disorientation that many schools experience today results from the crisis in the institutional program of the modern school form; a crisis that manifests itself as inefficiency in the face of the demands of a new sociocultural context where the distinguishing features are complexity, cultural diversity, respecting individual differences, and social integration under a new form of citizenry.

However, disillusionment and impotence cannot be built into the definitive response to the program's crisis. We need to make commitments to overcome the crisis atmosphere and develop more equitable, efficient, and respectful schooling. In this, alternative *project pedagogy* and the contract replace the old institutional program. As Jacques Donzelot has indicated, although the program founds public action on the previous definitions of a certain number of operations and submits a general content valid everywhere, the project is specific to a particular location and to the actions of its individual promoters. Therefore, it adapts to local circumstances and "proposes a comprehensive focus that restores each question to the complex set it is part of" (1994, 41). The program originates from an imposition; the project originates from the commitment of all players involved.

The form of schooling that arises on the basis of the educational project's philosophy is a result of reviewing internal issues in the school organization itself, as well as external issues affecting the relationship with the social setting it becomes part of. In terms of internal issues, the educational project attaches importance to the individual's vantage point by placing the subject in the center of the pedagogical relationship. But "the subject is not the individual, and nothing else; the subject is not the passive object of relationship, but its protagonist, an autonomous and solitary protagonist" (Terrén 2003, 265).

It must be remembered that the players the school makes an appeal to are no longer "students"; they are "subjects" who not only recover the conscious world with isolated socialization agencies as starting point, but they "construct" their social reality by conjugating the multiple experiences they acquire in the various contexts in which they interact with others. As subjects are obviously active in the construction of their vital project, the form of schooling cannot be limited to the mere transfer of knowledge and inherited and programmed models of interpretation. Conversely, the school must transmit the skills necessary to construct or produce independent knowledge that arises from egalitarian dialogue among all those involved in the training process (Aubert et al. 2004, 124–25).

In terms of external issues that attack the traditional school form emanating from the idea of the project, perhaps the most relevant are those referring to the new frontiers of the now-secularized sanctuary. When the legitimacy of the school is no longer "sacred," it has to be democratic. This comes to mean something beyond exposing the work in the classroom to different points of view. It entails the active involvement of students, teachers, and parents[6] in the educational and management dynamics of the classroom. Likewise, the democratic legitimacy of the sanctuary must also entail its opening to the surrounding community in an attempt to break through the demarcation between formal, and nonformal-and-informal education. This boundary no longer makes sense when subjects are considered, from an all-encompassing perspective, as active subjects constructing their vital projects based on all contexts of interaction they participate in. From this comprehensive perspective, the training space transcends the classroom and the training task is no longer exclusive to the faculty.

Socioeducational Action in the World: A Communicative Study

With these theoretical premises as starting point, by initiative of a group of researchers from the Department of Sociology 2 at the Universidad del País Vasco /Euskal Herriko Unibertsitatea (UPV/EHU, University of the Basque Country), we and others began meeting as persons from various academic disciplines and professional experiences, with an interest in contributing to the betterment of the situation of disadvantaged social groups. A task force, Koheslan (Kohesio Soziala Lantzen, Cultivating Social Cohe-

---

6. The involvement of parents is essential for purposes of generating the social capital necessary in disadvantaged sectors that find difficulties with networking, cooperation, and developing intercultural and interpersonal confidence, which is the foundation of solid social integration.

sion), resulted from this series of encounters and a research project was developed, "Roma and Basque Immigrants in Their Adolescent Life Cycle."[7]

The study took place in three stages between 2004 and 2008. In the first phase, the project was defined as an experience in communication between different forms of knowledge, some in the academic realm, such as sociology to a large degree, but also anthropology and pedagogy, and others in the realm of intervention, such as education at school, social education, and volunteering. The intention was to see a broad ranging view of the situation of Roma and immigrant adolescents in Basque society.

The overall goal was *detecting opportunities* for adolescents and youth living in situations of unequality and social rejection to *display their capabilities*. In this sense, we should clarify that we were not placing ourselves in front of individuals with successful academic learning histories, or in front of socially brilliant projects in terms of an academic, occupational, or work-related future, but in front of *quality life projects* (Martínez Domínguez 2002), with the understanding that a quality life requires *confidence*—or material and affective security—and *recognition*, of its unique contribution. Thus, the general hypothesis that guided the study stated that *the satisfactory development of the life project in minority adolescents involves a multiplicity of interactions, and confidence and recognition practices,* starting from an educational project that transcends the realm of the pedagogical relationship of the school by involving the adolescent's social and family environment.

In this first stage, we initiated the school context approach by holding interviews with the administrators of the nine selected schools.[8] Their

---

7. The research team consisted of Roma community members and immigrants well known for their commitment and professional activities, expert agents in education and pedagogy, and finally, university professors and researchers from various academic disciplines. In addition, the team received technical assistance from associations and agencies that enriched the research with specific contributions. Worthy of special mention is the involvement of Basque schools. The study was possible thanks to cofunding from the Vice-Chancellor's Office of Research at the UPV/EHU and the Basque Government's Departments of Education and Well-Being. Given the limited space for presenting, from this point on we will explain the basic elements of the study with regards to the immigrants' case, and leave for another time the treatment in the case of adolescents of Roma ethnicity whose specificity requires a particular individualized treatment.

8. The Fundación Peñascal Fundazioa vocational school, and the secondary schools Artaza-Romo, Gurutzeta, Mungia and Txurdinaga-Behekoa in Bizkaia; the Francisco de Vitoria secondary school and El Carmen adult education school in Araba; and the Bidebieta, and Koldo Mitxelena secondary schools in Gipuzkoa.

cooperation achieved two functions of great importance to the study: first, connecting the study with the adolescents whose profiles matched plan needs, as well as their families; second, participating in the process of interpreting the dialogue maintained with the adolescents.

Immigrant students receive their schooling for the most part in urban settings, and to a much lesser extent in semi-urban settings. Their most common place of origin is Latin America (Ecuador and Colombia at the top of the list), followed by Africa (Morocco and Sub-Saharan countries); yet there are also groups of European (Portugal and Romania), and finally Asian (mostly from China) origin. Essentially due to the recent arrival of immigrants to the Basque Country, a large part of them are students in the lower division of compulsory secondary education, although they are gradually reaching the second division, and to a lesser extent post-secondary or vocational schools. The "age gap" on the part of these students is a consequence of the "curricular gap." This occurs because of the difficulty in adapting to a new social and academic context, differences in the curriculum, and often-deficient schooling in their countries of origin. The main obstacle they need to overcome is cultural, social, and academic adaptation, and different forms linguistic adaptation.

Most schools feel ready—or are in the process of becoming ready—to provide an adequate response to typical problems of school adaptation, motivation to study, and acquisition of the basic elements of learning. A range of measures are deployed along these lines, aimed at addressing educational needs related to diversity. The most developed measures seek to provide educational reinforcement to students with schooling difficulties so that after a first implementation of individualized reinforcement outside the classroom, progress can be made toward formats within the group or outside regular school hours, avoiding forms of segregation to the greatest extent possible. In general, schools place a positive value on the effects of these measures, as well as the resources obtained from management in order to implement them. Nevertheless, it is increasingly felt that management sets forth very specific guidelines that in practice limit the autonomy to carry out in-house projects. They also notice a lack of concurrency between different administrations and different services when it comes time to address problems and respond to demands. In fact, some participating schools have become *Learning Communities*[9] that are

---

9. Such being the case of the secondary school in the municipality of Mungia (Munguía).

commited to a greater mutual involvement between teachers, families, and interactive local groups.

In its second phase the study reviewed the biographical backgrounds of the stakeholders in their compulsory schooling stage, or recent departure from this stage, taking into account age, socioeconomic situation, ethnicity, and gender, as hypothetical indicators of exclusion.[10] The goal in this stage of the study was to determine under what circumstances those indicators become barriers to inclusion. But the study was exploring mainly in reverse, in other words, the hidden or denied reality of skills and capabilities with a great potential in current society, and how the protagonists, when in the presence of given favorable circumstances, transform them into opportunities to overcome exclusion. For this, we decided to adopt the communicative approach of biographies in dialogue format or life storytelling (Bertaux 1997), which required us to set up multiple paths, in addition to taking care of face-to-face exchanges, in situ interactions, communications in the field, in order to achieve the transformative dialogue that is part of the *critical communicative methodology* in social research (Gómez et al. 2006).

The second phase concluded with a diagnosis about the subject's situation and the practices and interactions that helped them make progress in their life projects. Results confirmed that the satisfactory development of the life project for immigrant adolescents involves a multiplicity of interactions and practices of confidence and recognition as factors of inclusion. In the diagnosis, we noticed that different agencies and agents—family members, educators, social welfare caseworkers or professionals, and civil associations—share responsibility in the task of making quality life projects possible. We pointed out that when all these entities become coordinated and cooperate as a network on behalf of this youth, developing together with them multiple interactions that transmit confidence and recognition, their self-esteem improves as well as their expectations for the present and the future.

In this regard, during the third phase we considered the "environment" as a socioeducational setting for social cohesion; in other words,

---

10. A total of twenty-one in-depth interviews took place with adolescents. With input from them and those closest to them—their teachers, family members or community educators on the street—a diagnosis was developed that included daily practices and interactions having a positive impact on their paths.

the life setting where the adolescents find their opportunities for group and personal growth within common society. In this setting we sought *cooperative practices between school context, social welfare context, and family context.* For this purpose we interviewed people responsible for social services, community street educators, families, and immigrant grassroots activists, at two local areas selected because of the diversity of their sociological features, situated in the municipalities of Mungia (rural-urban) and District 1 of Vitoria-Gasteiz (urban).[11]

By focusing our interest in the socioeducational practices of a student's surroundings we addressed practices that think and produce surroundings. This is never a given, as if it were a natural fact, but just the opposite, it takes shape by means of the community cooperation practices. This explains why, in our case, we considered "surroundings" as a socioeducational setting; in other words, the setting in life where opportunities for growth are found by reason of the setting's multiplicity of interactions.

The results obtained show us that although some of these practices are general in nature, and therefore can often be extended to adolescents of any background, other practices instead are more directly linked to the migrant status of the adolescents of either gender participating in the study. Next, we will summarize under two categories: diversity and idenpendence practices and training and guidance practices

---

11. The *IES Mungia BHI* is located in the municipality of Mungia, near Bilbao (Bizkaia). The continuous growth of the Mungia population during the twentieth century is due to the evolution from a rural economy to an industrial and tertiary economic system. By midcentury the population was around 5,000; in the year 2002 it reached 14,000 indicating a trend contrary to the rest of Bizkaia and the Basque Country as a whole. In recent years, the percentage of the population represented by immigrants has increased. In 1998 it was 6.21 percent and reached 21.14 percent in 2001. The majority of immigrants come from Latin America, particularly Colombia (47.75 percent), most of them women, which is the opposite for persons coming from Morocco (9.01 percent). Likewise, District 1 in Vitoria-Gasteiz consists of four neighborhoods: *La Almendra* in the old quarter; the Ensanche or area outside the old quarter developed during the nineteenth-century expansion; and two neighborhoods that arose from the intake of immigrants arriving from other communities in the Spanish state near the middle of the twentieth century, Coronación in the 1960s and El Pilar in the 1970s. One third (30.64 percent) of foreign nationals in the city lives in these neighborhoods, with a positive migratory balance between 1997 and 2006. In terms of the different immigrant communities in Vitoria-Gasteiz, they mostly originate in Colombia (2,300), followed by Morocco (2,058), Algeria (1,120) and Ecuador (1,117). The *IES Francisco de Vitoria BHI* school, located in the neighborhood of El Pilar, receives a large portion of these students.

Diversity and Independence Practices

The form of being together practiced by adolescents is to a large extent a unique experience, while outside of the parents' control. Their experiential euphoria traverses, at times, ambivalent spheres between a family and a school that are no longer what they used to be. As these two major influences lose their ability to contain social life and give it meaning, subject's perceive deficiencies in a social services system designed for homogeneity and routine (Fantova 2006). A symptomatic complaint by social work professionals (including volunteers) is that they need to deal with issues that greatly exceed their capabilities; even so, they are able to achieve meritory practices in very conflictive situations.

There is much to be learned from these fragmented experiences, because they remind us to what extent it becomes necessary to *make a solid commitment to social services that reflect clear goals, incorporated into school, family, and community networks*, and well equipped with human and material resources. Beyond the necessary intervention in situations of imminent risk, preventive work directed at the adolescent universe is usually the true Achilles' heel of social services. It is essential to make community resources available to adolescent youth; for example, to organize during their free time workshops that they themselves ask for. There is a need to streamline the *establishment of support networks* that mitigate the negative effects of broken homes, bad school experiences, community rejection, or racist or xenophobic surroundings where the most punished are banished to high risk spaces.

Be accompanied and keep company. Given the multiplicity of essential transitions that migrant adolescents undergo, from before through after their departure, as well as the uncertainties about their future, *being accompanied* takes on huge relevance. Having available support from the family is essential but insufficient, because the family itself initial suffers similar deficiencies. Companionships *must be diversified in order to be effective* in material terms as well as moral, symbolic, and affective terms; thus, schools, civic associations, and social services, need to work cooperatively, in the interests of achieving a level of reliability capable of supporting their vital projects. In addition to being accompanied, *keeping company* is of major importance among adolescents, and even greater in the case of new arrivals who are deprived of their earlier friendships, with the resulting feeling of irreparable loss and loneliness. The bonds of friendship are based on extended *affinities* understood in the broadest sense: cultural, religious, or experiential. In any case, solidifying a *friend-ship network* at a particular location is a powerful factor for setting roots at that place, to the extent of it becoming an anchor for remaining there (Davila Legeren and García Santiago 2007).

The school usually facilitates the best opportunities for initial con-tacts, which can also take place in the neighborhood or in town, through sports, for example. *Sports activities* provide opportunities for young men and women of different schools, neighborhoods or towns, to share an experience, foster cooperation and support, and even *make friendships*. It is especially important to make sure that *gender inequality does not become perpetuated in this type of relationship* (such as soccer being the "king of sports," or in open spaces such as the streets, where the male position is dominant). Finally, it is important to develop *spaces for interaction, such as shared-activities workshops*, using as starting points for adolescents of both genders their own interests and affinities, as well as *the diversity and open and permeable nature of friendship networks* that each adolescent becomes involved in.

Learning the language. Young male and female immigrants may encounter communication difficulties on the street and at school, espe-cially in the first few years. In some cases the difficulty stems from not knowing the dominant language (Basque, Spanish, or both); in other cases it is due to the lack of comprehension of alien paraverbal forms—tones, rhythms, emphasis—which makes it difficult to cross the threshold from routine communication to the more formalized language involved in the school process (Vila 2005).

It is essential *for the school to provide support in the language field*, especially in the first few years of schooling, thus contradicting the cli-ché that adolescents learn languages almost without realizing it. It is important that schools provide newcomers *clear information on the importance of knowing both official languages of the community,* for pur-poses of their inclusion as equals as well as consistency in society, and at the same time offer them *resources so that this learning process can take place with quality assurance.* In the case of adolescents of foreign origin established within predominantly Spanish-speaking sociolinguis-tic contexts (as in the case of Vitoria-Gasteiz), it becomes difficult for them to understand the symbolic and practical usefulness of the Basque language, Euskara, which requires multiple and coherent efforts to pro-mote the language jointly from the environment. In Basque-speaking or mixed contexts (as in the case of Mungia) the need becomes more evident for coordinated action—between schools, local social services, and language promoting associations—addressing the advancement and support of a *sociolinguistic environment adequate for the inclusion of newcomers.*

Security in identity and social cohesion. Cultural difference should be converted into a positive attribute—worthy of occupying a common place in equality—with the added benefit of allowing a nonstigmatized personal experience of the origin itself. Paradoxically, security in identity of origin guarantees an opening to the knowledge and acquisition of surrounding cultural features, as well as transformation. Therefore, it is not a goal for emigrating adolescents to become nothing other than just immigrants, thus mitigating the tension that makes them be who they are. The life richness potentially made possible by the double condition that distinguishes them as migrants is something they come to feel gradually, until they state with satisfaction their own ambivalence "I feel I am from here and from there," a double condition that, instead of a deficiency, can be an added opportunity.

On this note, scheduled activities—*from the immigrants' association, from the school, or from the social center*—that seek a gratifying experience from multicultural social interaction, have the power to shatter stereotypes, giving everyone the opportunity to use and enjoy the best features in each. *Activities scheduled jointly by "native" and "foreign" persons* serve as experiment for those involved, and for others as an example of what the education is, in freedom and equity, that they preach. In activist work *networks of help and support* are gradually developed, and are especially necessary in those times and/or places where the quality life project of the migrant adolescent appears to be shrinking away.

No gender discrimination. The school curriculum should avoid replicating approaches toward the future that only call for young women to perform those *roles that are socially assigned to women, and in particular migrant women*; these roles almost always involve providing caregiving services to other people, either in public settings, teaching, health care, and so on, or in private settings, for families and in services. It is also important to make sure such gender-oriented approaches are not replicated when providing workshops or courses in community services. Finally, it is essential to undertake throughout the socioeducational setting, a *democratic management of the space* so that it is not taken over by the young men. There needs to be a strong awareness of the fact that on the street and in open spaces usually the young male is in charge; therefore, it is important to fight against the exclusionary attitudes arising from this situation. Throughout the entire socioeducational setting for the adolescent, it is necessary to schedule *leisure, sporting, and entertainment activities that satisfy adolescents from different origins and of either gender*, favoring the development of mixed groups.

Recreation through dialogue. The social significance of age occurs in space and time. Migrant youth notice differences between age representations in their places of origin and those prevalent in their current society. Certain gaps stand out, such as their time for training becoming longer, and the independence in managing spaces and leisure time. As we have seen, many young people see an increase in their freedom of movement, facilitated through mediation and dialogue. It is beneficial to all parties that teachers and social educators come to terms with *negotiating the conditions of freedom for adolescents together with parents willing to engage in dialogue*. It is also beneficial that adolescents are able to *engage in dialogue about forms of recreation* with the purpose of *seeking, from mutual respect, maximum contact among adolescents of various origins.*

Training and Guidance Practices

Migrant adolescents assume they require a good level of training to fulfill the working future set forth on the road map followed by their parents. This path needs incentives, a high level of training, and continuous guidance. *High expectations* encourage adolescents to face the difficulties that advancing their projects entails; this makes them realize how necessary it is, on the one hand, to acquire skills and abilities for communicating and for teamwork, and on the other hand a *good technical level of training and cross-training.*

Family support of the adolescent child's comprehensive training. A priority concern of migrant parents is to ensure a good schooling for their sons and daughters. This involves, on the one hand, providing them with sufficient material resources, and on the other hand, accompanying them throughout the process. The parents' commitment to *improving their own training by means of adult education*, serves as an exemplary factor to their children.

Interculturality. In the context of social well-being, it is important for the different cultures the adolescents partake in to be present at the school as well as in the community. This presence is sought in different forms and at different times—at the moment of intake and welcome, when introducing new students, during intercultural weeks, at festivities—although what is truly important is *for interculturality to be a constant element in the school curriculum as well as in scheduling social services*, so that they reflect a positive meaning attributed to the diversity of origins and therefore contribute to social cohesion.

The virtues of the policy of *porosity of the walls* between the classroom—as well as the actual school—and the social life outside, appear to be clear in the new multicultural realities; this policy involves agents circulating in both directions. It is important to situate young migrants in the world of standards to which they have arrived—to the extent of being able to make it their own and participate in its transformation—and likewise for them to feel recognized in terms of their differences. Equally important is to *support their cosmopolitan concerns* by encouraging them to carry out their travel fantasies through reading, audiovisual materials, surfing the web, or actual travel.

Findings: Educating in the Public Sphere

Through the various phases of the study mentioned, it has been possible to verify, from the youths' standpoint as well as from the standpoint of school-based and non-school-based educators, how the process of achieving a quality life project and the social inclusion of young immigrants of both genders requires going beyond those measures that exclusively affect the pedagogical relationship. The value of these measures is not denied, nor the effort on the part of the administration to involve resources for their advancement. What is made clear is their insufficiency or, in other words, the need to leverage other measures that, through holistic approaches, allow cross-linking formal and nonformal education in an integrated educational project within the youth's social and community setting.

This type of approach requires a reformulation of the sites for education, which extend beyond the spaces for training, as well as redefining the agents involved in the educational process. In fact, it makes it necessary for educational agents to proceed beyond the limits of their safety net in order to encounter within the community individuals as well as educational, cultural, sporting, or relief organizations, with the intention of developing a cooperative network in the process of preparing a *Community-Based Educational Plan*.

The development of a plan of this nature begins once it is assumed that: the education of the adolescent does not conclude with the *time* at school, but takes place during school time, family time, and free time, and educational action must seek a continuity between these three periods of time. Furthermore, the adolescent's education does not only include the *space* at school; traversing multiple spaces is particularly typical of adolescence and educational action should encourage the "educational use" of various spaces. Finally it is imperative to recognize that we are all *educators* and *learners*; through interaction we play both roles at the same time and we should consequently promote "educational volunteerism" and "participation."

With the cooperation of individuals active in the community, the educational plan sets forth a *sequence of initiatives*: thoroughly study and learn the cultural and social dynamics taking place in the community; encourage dialogue between local agents and agencies involved in adolescents' education; schedule educational sessions that seek to promote attitudes and practices of mutual trust and recognition within a common ground; promote knowledge of the similarities as well as the differences (in age, ethnicity, gender) of all individuals in the local community; encourage participation in joint ventures by various subjects (for example, the common effort to revitalize Euskara as a language of use); address a movement to develop and train adult family members that would have favorable repercussions on the education of their minor children; establish strategies to fight against academic failure and to facilitate professional guidance; take priority and exceptional steps in connection with youth and families facing great risk of social marginalization; capture local human resources that can move within the various youth education spaces; attract nonlocal agents (university affiliated or others) to participate in the development of the specific local dynamics of the plan; and any other aimed at making possible a quality life for the younger members of the community.

Of course, the growing commitment by public bodies to contribute to the development of this type of experiences is going to be essential. For this to occur, the various administrations must understand that their involvement in these experiences cannot be governed by the comings and goings of political jurisdiction, but by the principle of cooperation.

References

Abad Miguélez, Begoña. 2009. "Juventud, inmigración y acción educativa." Paper presented at the XVII Congreso de Estudios Vascos. Innovación para el Progreso Social Sostenible, Vitoria-Gasteiz, 18, 19 and 20 of November.

Arriaga Landeta, Mikel. 2007. "El entorno local como ámbito de acción socioeducativa." *Zerbitzuan* 42: 61–73.

Aubert, Adriana, Elena Duque, Montserrat Fisas and Rosa Valls. 2004. *Dialogar y transformar. Pedagogía crítica del siglo XXI.* Barcelona: Graó.

Bertaux, Daniel. 1997. *Les récits de vie. Perspective ethnosociologique.* Paris: Nathan.

Calero, Jorge. 2006. *La equidad en educación. Informe analítico del sistema educativo español.* Madrid: Centro de Investigación y Documentación Educativa (CIDE).

Davila Legeren, Andrés, and Oihane García Santiago. 2007. "El acompañamiento. Un factor básico de inclusión del menor migrante." Paper presented at the IX Congreso Español de Sociología, Barcelona, September, 13–15.

Donzelot, Jacques. 1994. *L'État animateur: Essai sur la politique de la ville.* Paris: Esprit.

Dubet, Françoise. 2003. "Mutaciones cruzadas: la ciudadanía y la escuela." In *Aprendiendo a ser ciudadanos: Experiencias sociales y construcción de la ciudadanía entre los jóvenes,* edited by María Luz Morán and Jorge Benedicto, Madrid: Injuve.

Elboj, Carmen, Ignasi Puigdellivol, Marta Soler, and Rosa Valls. 2002. *Comunidades de aprendizaje. Transformar la educación.* Barcelona: Graó.

Fantova, Fernando. 2006. "Algunos elementos para un análisis de las políticas sobre servicios sociales en el País Vasco." *Zerbitzuan* 40: 7–20.

Flecha, Ramón. 2009. "The Educative City and Critical Education." In *The Routledge International Handbook of Critical Education,* edited by Michael W. Apple, Wayne Au, and Luis Armando Gandia. New York & London: Routledge Taylor & Francis.

Gómez, Jesús, Antonio Latorre, Montse Sánchez, and Ramón Flecha. 2006. *Metodología comunicativa crítica.* Barcelona: El Roure.

Henriot-Van Zanten, Agnés. 1994. "Les politiques éducatives municipales: un example de mobilisation locales des acteurs de l'éducation." In *L'École et le territoire: nouveaux espaces, nouveaux enjeux*, edited by Bernard Charlot, Paris: Armand Colin.

Koheslan. 2005. *Gitanos e inmigrantes vascos en su ciclo de vida adolescente. Un proyecto de investigación comunicativa.* Bilbao: UPV/EHU.

———. 2006. *Gitanos e inmigrantes vascos en su ciclo de vida adolescente (2). Un diagnóstico de sentido.* Bilbao: UPV/EHU.

———. 2008. *Gitanos e inmigrantes vascos en su ciclo de vida adolescente (3). Hacia un plan socioeducativo en el entorno.* Bilbao: UPV/EHU.

Lapeyronnie, Didier. 1992. "Les politiques locales d'intégration des immigrés en Europe." In *Immigrés en Europe: politiques locales d'intégration*, edited by Didier Lapeyronnie. Paris: La Documentation Française.

Martínez Domínguez, Begoña. 2002. *La educación en la diversidad en los albores del siglo XXI.* Barcelona: Paidós.

Marchesi, Álvaro. 2006. "El informe PISA y la política educativa en España." *Revista de Educación.* Número extraordinario: 337–55.

Terrén, Eduardo. 2003. "Educación democrática y ciudadanía multicultural: el reaprendizaje de la convivencia." In *Aprendiendo a ser ciudadanos. Experiencias sociales y construcción de la ciudadanía entre los jóvenes*, edited by María Luz Morán and Jorge Benedicto. Madrid: Injuve.

Vila, Ignasi. 2005. "¿Nivel sociocultural o desconocimiento de la lengua?" *Perspectiva CEP* 8: 23–54.

8

Educating from the Family: A Proposal to Connect Homes and Institutions

ENRIQUE ARRANZ FREIJO, FERNANDO OLABARRIETA ARTETXE,
and JUAN LUIS MARTÍN AYALA

There is a current historical phenomenon that involves pressure exerted by the socioeconomic system on the process of child upbringing: the duty to provide for basic needs in terms of food and shelter—and a society of comfort that demands high levels of consumption—makes it impossible for young couples to devote suitable time and resources to the education of their children. Moreover, sociologists (Flaquer 1998) identify an unstoppable process of *institutionalization of family functions*; this context includes all those social services initiatives aimed at alleviating deficiencies in dysfunctional families, such as foster care and adoption services. There are also institutional services that perform traditionally family-based functions, such as child care and elder care. These include the implementation of education for ages zero to three and for elders, senior residences, and senior day care. Certainly a dialectic process is taking place of *institutionalization of the family* and *familiarization of the institutions*.

Often there is mention in the media that the lack of commitment toward education on the part of parents explains issues of growing concern to society, such as violence and academic failure, drug usage, teen pregnancies, and so on. Far from a stance of blaming parents, a solution should be offered to parents that serves the function, on the one hand, of reminding them that when it comes to providing certain needs to a human being in development—such as unconditional love and to practice necessary demands—their role as parents is irreplaceable, and on the other hand, provide them with guidelines and educational resources so they can assuredly perform their nurturing roles. It should also be noted that the traditional benchmarks for family education, rooted in the undisputable authority of the father or the parents and in religious values, are in a crisis stage in a more egalitarian and more secular society.

This fact mandates an appropriate replacement of those benchmarks, because children can and should be educated. The proposed route is for families to absorb the academic knowledge that has demonstrated its efficiency in the development of healthy attitudes and skills for peaceful coexistence and the respect of basic human rights. Quite distant from conservative stances that defend the family institution as guarantor of traditional values, it is felt that the family should be supported and strengthened by institutions and reclaimed as an educational agent for the citizenry. In this sense, there is a need for policies of greater depth than simply financial support, so as to facilitate family coexistence, the development of families, and compatibility between the domains of family and work.

Our research idea arose from a counseling service for families within the research group on family contexts and psychological development within the Basic Psychological Processes and their Development section of the Department of Psychology at the Universidad del País Vasco/Euskal Herriko Unibertsitatea (UPV/EHU, University of the Basque Country). Between 2001 and 2003 the team developed a research project titled "Assessment of Quality in Family Interaction and Psychological Development in Children Ages Five and Eight from the Autonomous Community of the Basque Country: Grounds for a Proposal for the Training of Parents." During the execution of the project, the research team designed a protocol for the assessment of family contexts (Arranz et al. 2004; Arranz 2005; Arranz and Oliva 2010) that used as a core reference Urie Bronfenbrenner's ecological model (1979, 2005; Bronfenbrenner and Morris, 1998). This protocol allowed the team to delineate the optimum family context for purposes of facilitating a healthy psychological development in children, and it helped profile one of the cornerstones of the service proposal: its preventive and educational nature. It was necessary to create an awareness of the conditions of that optimum family context, and likewise to provide mentorship to parents so that they would be able to implement it in their homes; this was the primary prevention premise in the service's design.

A preventive and educational focus required conveying a perception of the service as something different from a clinical-type office where one could receive counseling on psychological pathologies. It was very important to create awareness that any family could inquire about any specific problem or educational issue without the need to be suffering some serious condition. In any case, the service also provided an important function in terms of early detection of specific problems and their referral to other competent services or professionals in each instance.

When it came to deciding which could be the avenues for offering the service, the team felt that it should be offered from public institutions to families. By doing so, the families would have access to certain resources that are currently offered mainly in the private sector. This working team feels that the implementation of preventive and educational psychological services should be public in nature, and should run in parallel—not in competition against but as a complement to other types of services, such as health services.

Perhaps the greatest challenge the working team faced was to find the formula for making the service available to families. Obviously there was a need to move past the traditional format of parenting schools, which are usually lectures given by an expert, or group workshops on educational topics usually presented in schools. That format is effective and enables some families to develop and make considerable progress as educators. Nevertheless, there are many families that are unable or lack the motivation to attend those activities, or perhaps they dare not reveal in public the real issue that concerns them; moreover, they do not consult a professional so as to maintain privacy or due to a lack of financial resources or information.

The solution to the stated problems appeared when considering the possibility of offering the service by telephone, and later by e-mail; this forces the inquiring family to state the issue of concern in writing, thus helping to identify it, contextualize it, and make a specific inquiry from the service team. In addition, e-mail makes it possible to maintain an interactive sequence between the family and the service until each case is guided, and allows subsequent follow-up of the case. This communication has the advantages of immediate accessibility, confidentiality, and individualized contact, and is effective in a process of initial mentoring in connection with various issues; it will never replace the direct relationship between the specialist and the individual, which is required in therapeutic processes.

It is important to learn to what extent future users—mothers and fathers—search online for information pertaining to their children's education. If the search term "*escuela de padres*" (parents' school) is entered in a search engine, the result is that 99,800 pages contain the term; in the case of the term "parenting" the number of pages grows to 49,100,000. These figures show a high demand for information on the part of parents; as indicted by Nicholas Long (2004)—in the most significant text published to date on the topic of "e-parenting"—the demand for information on family education has been growing incrementally, although not as impressively as searching the net for information on health.

Overwhelmingly these pages offer information to families about child upbringing; some of them come from private individuals, others from schools or various cultural or religious institutions; some of them offer the possibility of a consultation on specific issues with specialists. Not all pages are of equal quality in content, from the standpoint of being based on academic and educational criteria; some of them are guided by ideological or religious principles without an academic counterpoint. In fact, one of the functions of the Etxadi service project consists of processing this broad-ranging information, identifying and selecting valuable content and screening out lower-quality content, in order to provide appropriate information to the families.

The current historical moment is characterized by the continual unfolding of the new society of information. Javier Echeverría (1999) has given the name of "*tercer entorno*" (third environment) to this new context that people are gradually adapting to. Echeverría describes a process of humanization of the new technologies, and a process of computerization of human relations. In the family setting this dialectic process is evident: the family is becoming computerized and techno-savvy, and technologies are becoming familiar to the service of family relationships; one example is today's parents telemonitoring their children through the mobile phone. According to Echeverría, in the new *telepolis* the services that traditionally were in the hands of institutions will be entering homes through computer communication technology. The new "deterritorialized" space of *telepolis* is the location of support services to parents, offered by the Etxadi project.

The proposal by Etxadi (www.etxadi.org) for a service to families through the Internet has its origins in the field of mental health; specifically in the initiative by Epotec (www.epotec.com), a company that offers on-line information on mental health and preventive criteria, through the

Internet; it also offers individual mentoring and support, participation in discussion groups, and the possibility of participating in interactive groups dealing with issues such as anxiety, depression, phobias, interpersonal relations, and other programs focused on parenting topics. These programs consist of eight to ten sessions where participants have at their disposal a professional who guides them throughout the development of the program.

Within the still-emerging convergence of technologies, for example, between television and computer, Long (2004) describes the experience of the Canadian Institute of Child Health. With support from the Canadian government, the institute has developed the e-parenting network (www. eparentingnetwork.ca). This innovative multimedia network includes interactive television modules with information and training for parents in various issues such as safety, nutrition criteria, and positive parenting: parents can download information, submit inquiries to experts via e-mail, and access other pages with recommended content. The Parentline Plus (www.parentlineplus.org.uk) service is wide-ranging in the United Kingdom and is another example of Internet support provided to families on the topic of parenting.

There are many Spanish-language pages devoted to mothers and fathers; one of the higher quality ones has been developed by the Regional Government of Extremadura within its program for expansion of new technologies. The Virtual School for Mothers and Fathers of Extremadura (www.nccextremadura.org/portal/enredamos/escuela.htm) offers training materials to families, and the possibility of consultation on specific cases, which are handled by specialists.

The working team decided to also offer the counseling service on family education to the educators in the Haurreskolak consortium, the public educational network for children from zero to three years of age in the Comunidad Autónoma del País Vasco/Euskal Autonomia Erkidegoa (CAPV/EAE, Autonomous Community of the Basque Country). The purpose is to address inquiries from the staff of educators in order to provide them with the training and skills in mentoring criteria, in their connections with families with children between four months and two years of age.

The proposal from the working team is summarized in the following general goals:

- Offer parents a public service of counseling on family topics and on parenting children and youth

- Help improve family relations and psychological development in children
- Prevent the incidence of problems throughout childhood
- Timely detection of cases requiring specific treatment
- Provide information and specific and customized mentoring on daily problems in parenting children

In order for the above goals to be met, the families that would potentially use this consulting service should perceive it on the basis of the following premises:

- As a counseling service, nonpathological in nature, that can provide mentorship to facilitate a healthy psychological development in their children and to tackle issues pertaining to daily parenting situations: toilet training, temper tantrums, academic failure, shyness, relationship with teens, drug use prevention, facing the process of separation and divorce, and so on.
- As a service that is available, in close proximity, providing prompt support.
- As a customized and confidential service.
- As a useful resource that offers benefits without direct economic cost.

Immediate goals proposed for this work include the following:

- Implement the service in cooperation with various public institutions
- Analyze the quantitative response on the part of the families.
- Qualitatively analyze the family consultation topics.
- Analyze the quantitative response of the educational staff from the Haurreskolak consortium.[1]

Method

A description follows of the subjects participating in the experience, the implementation procedure, and the system for collecting data from the families.

The family mentoring service was made available to the families in those city and district authorities where a cooperation agreement was

---

1. For more information on the Haurreskolak consortium, see www.haurreskolak.net/ (information in Spanish and Basque).

reached. The families had free access to the service, and through the contact method of their choice. Access was accomplished by a total of 2,235 families.

The procedure used for implementing the mentoring service involved the following steps:

- Our team offered the service to interested communities and an agreement was reached through the university.

- Families are informed about how the service operates through local media including the press, television, radio, and other broadcast media customarily used by the procuring institution, which could be magazines, three-fold brochures, or others.

- Families are brought in to meet with the team providing the service; here a detailed presentation takes place of the service and all concerns expressed about its operation are addressed.

- Schools, health centers and other public places (cultural centers, social services) located in the service implementation area, especially pediatric services and early learning classrooms, are notified of its existence and the possibility of sending to it referrals dealing with specific questions on family-based childhood education.

- On a quarterly basis the Etxadi team publishes a parenting newsletter; which is sent to all families using the service. This general interest document deals with matters such as tips for educating on ethics, learning about limits, how to face the process of a couple breaking up, keys for a democratic education style.

- Families express their concerns preferably in writing by e-mail, postal mail, or initially by telephone contact. There is also an anonymous form on Etxadi web page that can be filled out with individualized family details.

- Within five working days the family receives an appropriate response to the query or concern expressed. Should there be a need to expand on the information, the mentoring team contacts the family, and if the situation so requires, a personal interview takes place.

- The responses provided to the families contain specific guidelines for taking steps in connection with the problem expressed; generic information is also offered on the topic in question so that families can increase their knowledge about this matter, and finally biographical references and online resources are offered to enable families to consult other relevant materials related to the topic of inquiry. The academic direction of the responses is eclectic within a systemic, organic, interactive, educational, and developmental theoretical framework (Arranz et al. 2004).

- Once the family has received the response, periodic follow-up takes place in order to assess the effectiveness of the response. The family fills out a questionnaire that includes their assessment of the response and the mentoring received. Thus an interactive process opens up between the family and the Etxadi team, aimed at the family becoming skilled as an educating entity that, together with the team, seeks solutions and strategies in order to face daily parenting tasks.
- Every three months the Etxadi team prepares a report on the operations of the service, and meets with technical teams from the procuring institutions in order to jointly assess the topics under inquiry and usage rate of the service. Short-term expansion plans are also prepared.

In schools, the service:
- Offers a family mentoring service through the school.
- The service to schools offers the possibility of performing preventive family assessments starting with the group comprising ages zero through three years old.
- Offers training seminars in order to provide skills for faculty to interact with families. Training seminars are also offered to train families.
- Offers consulting via Internet, aimed at solving teachers' concerns in connection with child behavior and daily interaction with families. This service is offered to teachers in the Haurreskolak consortium.
- The service aimed at families and educators is offered by a group of professionals and university specialists with doctorates in psychology and multidisciplinary training in the fields of education and mental health.

Family inquiries take place either through the contact phone, by postal mail, and through the service gateway located on the right side of the page providing access to the service. Each city hall, district authority, or institution has its own logo that provides access to the questionnaire that families submitting inquiries must fill out as mandatory. When in inquiry submitted so requires, the mentoring team requests additional information in order to be able to craft an appropriate response tailored to the uniqueness of each family.

Outcomes

Descriptive outcomes appear below, in connection with using the service during the time frames for implementation pertinent to each institution that has contracted for it:

The service has been offered to a wide range of institutions in the CAPV/EAE. The districts (mancomunidades/mankomunitateak) of Lea-Artibari and Urola-Garaia are groups of small ayuntamientos/udaletxeak (city halls) in the provinces of Bizkaia and Gipuzkoa, respectively. The first is a primarily rural area that includes some major fishing towns. The second is an industrial area with some rural enclaves.

Irun in Gipuzkoa (Larrañaga et al. 2005) and Portugalete in Bizkaia are mid-size towns, of middle and lower-middle socioeconomic background. They were formed by working families and received immigrant families (from elsewhere in the Spanish state) during the 1960s and also currently receive migrant populations from abroad. The Bilbao city hall is the largest in the Basque Country and its socioeconomic structure is quite diverse.

It was found that the languages used for inquiries was Euskara in nearly 27 percent of cases, with Spanish used for the remaining 73 percent. Contact was most often made by e-mail (49.22 percent), followed by phone (48.55 percent), and then postal mail (2.23 percent). Table 8.1 indicates the total number of families that could use the service and the actual number of inquiries made.

Table 8.1. Number of inquiries

	Number of potentially inquiring families	Number of inquiries
Lea-Artibai	1,562	637
Urola-Garaia	1,750	521
Irun	4,375	659
Portugalete	4,375	165
Bergara (Vergara)	1,000	144
Bilbao	23,666	119
Total	36,728	2,245

In table 8.2 we show subject matters of inquiry, broke into childhood and adolescence.

Table 8.2. Inquiries by ge group and subject matter in the mentoring service to families

Childhood		Adolescence	
Subject matter	Number (%)	Subject matter	Number (%)
Behavioral problems	220 (12.50%)	Behavioral problems	139 (31.30%)
Temper tantrums	178 (10.11%)	Drug and alcohol consumption	64 (14.41%)
Toilet training	161 (9.15%)	Going out at night	51 (11.48%)
Sleeping habits	146 (8.30%)	Motivation at school	29 (6.53%)
Jealousy	107 (6.08%)	Bibliography	28 (6.30%)
Problems with self-esteem and shyness	101 (5.74%)	Problems with self-esteem and shyness	18 (4.05%)
Eating habits	92 (5.23%)	Sexuality and sex education	16 (3.60%)
School performance and learning difficulties	79 (4.49%)	School performance and learning difficulties	12 (2.70%)
Rules and limitations	78 (4.43%)	Dealing with new technologies	9 (2.20%)
Phobias (Fears, fear of school, social fears)	53 (3.01%)	Social contacts	9 (2.20%)
Separation/Divorce	51 (2.89%)	Clinical problems	9 (2.20%)
Problems with language and bilingualism	49 (2.78%)	Depression and anxiety	8 (1.80%)
School adaptation	35 (1.98%)	Problems living together	8 (1.80%)
Academic motivation and homework	34 (1.93%)	Communication	7 (1.57%)
Illness or death in the family	33 (1.87%)	Rewards and punishment	5 (1.12%)
Bibliography	31 (1.76%)	Rules and limitations	5 (1.12%)
Rewards and punishment	28 1.59%)	Free time	4 (0.90%)
Depression and anxiety	26 (1.47%)	Harassment at school	3 (0.67%)
Extracurricular activities	26 (1.47%)	Responsibility	3 (0.67%)
Social contacts	24 (1.36%)	Separation/Divorce	3 (0.67%)
Pacifier and thumb-sucking	23 (1.30%)	Family conflict	2 (0.45%)
Hyperactivity and attention deficit	20 (1.13%)	Delinquent behaviors	2 (0.45%)
Dealing with new technologies	16 (0.90%)	Family stress	1 (0.22%)
Psychomotility	12 (0.68%)	Extracurricular activities	1 (0.22%)
Extended family	9 (0.51%)	Personality disorder	1 (0.22%)
Bonding	9 (0.51%)	Career guidance	1 (0.22%)
Responsibility	9 (0.51%)	Academic failure	1 (0.22%)
Harassment at school	8 (0.45%)	Falling in love	1 (0.22%)
Adoption	7 (0.39%)	Social skills	1 (0.22%)
Others	94 (5.34%)	Others	3 (0.67%)
Total	1759 (78.35%)		444 (21.65%)

In addition to the inquiries included on the tables, forty-two other queries were made, of which thirty-one dealt with information about the service or were from locales or institutions not participating in the mentoring program.

With regards to the Haurreskolak consortium teachers, from January 2006 until April 2009, 336 inquiries were received. Euskara was by far the language of choice (80.65 percent), followed by Spanish (19.35 percent). The percentage of e-mail inquires was also much higher (87.5 percent) versus phone (11.9 percent) and mail (0.6 percent). Table 8.3 shows the subject matter of the inquiries made by the teaching staff at the Haurreskolak consortium.

Table 8.3. Inquiry subject matters from faculty

Subject matter	Number (%)
Behavioral problems	51 (15.17%)
Developmental progress and psychomotility	33 (9.82%)
Eating habits	27 (8.03%)
Toilet training	26 (7.73%)
Biting and scratching	26 (7.73%)
Sleeping habits	19 (5.65%)
Bonding and dependency	16 (4.76%)
Information on courses and bibliography	15 (4.46%)
Adaptation period	14 (4.16%)
Temper tantrums	14 (4.16%)
Syndromes: Hyperactivity, special education needs, and others	9 (2.67%)
Communicating with families	8 (2.38%)
Problems with self-esteem	7 (2.08%)
Fears	6 (1.78%)
Pediatric topics and/or referrals	6 (1.78%)
Affective problems	5 (1.48%)
Emotional development	5 (1.48%)
Language problems	5 (1.48%)
School schedules and regulations	5 (1.48%)
Pacifier	4 (1.19%)
Training to families	4 (1.19%)
Punishment	4 (1.19%)
Play	3 (0.89%)
Cognitive development	3 (0.89%)
Rules and limitations	3 (0.89%)
Others	18 (5.35%)
Total	336

Discussion and Findings: Back to the Future

In terms of the goals stated earlier, it is worth mentioning from the quantitative standpoint that the information on usage of the service reflects an initial launching situation that needs to be solidified in the future. The frequency of service usage by families is satisfactory, considering the low penetration rates of online access services and the insufficient quality of the access available to many current users. An improved computer communication infrastructure will make possible a much more interactive and enriching relationship between the advising team and families, and among the families themselves.

The data do not yet allow a rigorous quantitative comparison between regions, because the timeframe for implementation, the dissemination strategy and the infrastructure for online access vary between the different regions. Nevertheless, the main language for inquiries is Spanish, and inquiries in the Basque language come primarily from small city halls. It has also been verified that close to 50 percent of inquiries have been via telephone, in spite of emphasizing to families that it is preferable to submit their concerns in writing and by e-mail. Also worth pointing out is the fact that the total number of inquiries is not identical to the number of families submitting inquires, because there is a group of families who pose inquiries from the service two or three times in connection with the same child or another of their children.

From the qualitative standpoint, the first significant fact is the percentage of questions on childhood (78.35 percent) and those referring to adolescence (21.65 percent). This could indicate a higher level of awareness for using the service between families with young children; in addition, a high percentage of queries refer to topics involving ages zero to two, because they deal with the acquisition of independent eating habits, toilet training, and sleeping. These topics are currently quite significant, since children begin entering schools starting at four months of age, just when they are acquiring habits of independence. Data on queries from the teaching staff at the Haurreskolak consortium verify the importance of this line of topics for the four-month-old through two-year-old age bracket. Obviously the acquisition of these first habits is currently an educational task shared between the family and the school. This highlights the need to develop seamless and effective communication protocols between parents and professional educators.

On the other hand it is noted that the highest percentages of queries, both in childhood and in adolescence, refer to the behavioral problems category where families are seeking mentorship or a solution to some specific concern. In this sense, families should be apprised of the possibility of consulting the service with a perspective that is preventive and empowering in terms of psychological development. From this standpoint, the second highest topic for inquiries from families in adolescence refers to drug and alcohol consumption; many of these inquiries require information on consumption behavior indicators and on strategies for addressing these issues when communicating with adolescents.

When submitting inquiries on childhood, the families' interest is evident when dealing with learning problems and strategies to effectively set forth rules and limitations in connection with family harmony. There is also a growing number of inquiries dealing with guidelines for steps in connection with separation and divorce proceedings; it seems that families are aware that these proceedings could affect the psychological development process and their concern is coping with this situation with standards of sound judgment.

As shown, the remaining topics of inquiry on the part of families is quite varied; this covers issues such as the use of two languages in a family setting, how to deal with specific traumatic situations such as the death of a family member, and new topics of growing interest such as the appropriate use of new technologies. Some consultations take place in connection with nonconventional family settings, such as adoption. There are also some inquiries on harassment at school.

There is a strange absence of queries dealing with sex education, both in childhood and adolescence. This gives the impression that families assume it is a topic dealt with developmentally and informatively at schools, when in reality it is covered quite sparsely, and with great variations in terms of depth of coverage in the standardized school curriculum. This is once again evidence of the need to identify the specific educational responsibilities of the family and the school, and the need to articulate coordinated efforts in those responsibilities that are shared.

In terms of the support service offered to teachers, results show behavioral problems in children as the main reason for the inquiry; this category includes those behaviors arising in the classroom and posing an immediate problem requiring a solution, such as aggression, social isolation, symptoms of depression, presence of negligence or family mistreatment indicators, and so on. Other reasons refer to independence habits and awareness of the evolutionary sequence of psychological development in order to weigh the age-appropriateness of certain behaviors. Early detection of special education needs in children also constitutes a reason for inquiry.

Other inquiries by educational professionals deal with communicating with families; educators require mentoring in order to carry out effective interviews with families; they also state the importance of having materials available to facilitate training families in topics dealing with parenting. In the case of Haurreskolak consortium educators, consulting with the Etxadi team also becomes a permanent online training tool.

The fact that it has been possible to implement a service with these features indicates a shift toward a perception of psychology and education as applied sciences of preventive benefit; in fact, the first institutions with sensitivity toward the proposal to provide families with support services were the social services for family intervention, from two groups of city halls. The same has been true of those institutions in the areas of education and culture. On behalf of Etxadi team, it is worth highlighting here the commitment to the future by the district authorities of Lea-Artibai and Urola-Garaia, and the city halls of Irun and Bergara in Gipuzkoa, as well as Portugalete and Bilbao in Bizkaia, pioneers in the implementation of the service. Starting in 2010, the city hall of Leioa (Lejona) in Bizkaia will also offer the service to its families, from the area of education.

The team's experience during these months has demonstrated that it is advisable, due to its novelty, to maintain a sustained publicity along a period of time so that parents can perceive the availability of the service. It is equally important to hold open meetings between parents and the persons providing the service in towns where it is offered; in this manner the families know who they are consulting, thus achieving a connection with greater trust and safety.

From the standpoint of assessing the benefit of the service, the overwhelming majority of families (97 percent) offer a positive assessment of the mentoring received, and especially the fact that the guidance is tailored to each particular case. Another matter quite difficult to approach methodologically is evaluating the actual effectiveness of the service as preventive intervention; looking at its effectiveness positively, the mentoring the team offers to families is based on comparative research results, and the ultimate goal of counseling is to empower parents as educators and providers of a family setting that favors a healthy psychological development.

The preventive approach should also be activated from the service itself, by making available to families materials of proven quality, in reference to various preventive settings. In this manner, the service will also be perceived as a continuous and updated training tool available to families, and there will be a contribution to the creation and dissemination of an authentic parenting culture.

Along the lines just suggested, it is worth mentioning the agreement reached at the City Hall Department for Youth, Education and Sport, in the Bilbao city hall for the Etxadi team to create a Web site in support of parents in their educational efforts. This Web site has been running since October 2006. Its contents can be accessed by visiting www.bilbao.net, and entering the section *Educar y Crecer en Familia/Familian hezi* (Family Education and Growth).

Recently, the team has finished developing a database on the inquiries submitted, as a survey and research analytical tool regarding the matters of interest to families in the various regions; all this aimed at structuring policies of preventive family intervention, based on actual data. Finally, since 2005, dissemination of the preliminary results of the family mentoring service implementation has been underway at national and international conferences (Manzano et al. 2005a, 2005b; Olabarrieta et al. 2009).

References

Arranz, Enrique. 2005. "Family Context and Psychological Development in Early Childhood: Educational Implications." In *Contemporary Perspectives on Families, Communities, and Schools for Young Children*, edited by Olivia N. Saracho and Bernard Spodeck. Greenwich, CT: Information Age Publishing.

Arranz, Enrique and Alfredo Oliva, coords. 2010. *Desarrollo psicológico en las nuevas estructuras familiares*. Madrid: Pirámide.

Arranz, Enrique, Alfredo Oliva, Águeda Parra, Amaia Azpiroz, Aranzazu Bellido, Raquel Malla, Ainoa Manzano, Juan Luis Martín, and Fernando Olbarrieta, Fernando. 2004. *Familia y desarrollo psicológico*. Madrid: Prentice Hall/Pearson Educación.

Bronfenbrenner, Urie. 1979. *The Ecology of Human Development: Experiments by Nature and Design*. Cambridge, MA: Harvard University Press.

———, ed. 2005. *Making Humans Being Human: Bioecological Perspectives on Human Development.* London: Sage Publications.

Bronfenbrenner, Urie, and Pamela A. Morris. 1998. "The Ecology of Developmental Processes." In *Handbook of Child Psychology.* Volume 1. *Theory*, edited by Richard M. Lerner. 5th ed. New York: Wiley.

Echeverría, Javier. 1999. *Los Señores del aire: telépolis y el tercer entorno.* Barcelona: Destino.

Flaquer, LLuis. 1998. *El destino de la familia.* Barcelona: Ariel.

Larrañaga, Maite, Ixiar Ezeiza, Nuria Galende, Ainoa Manzano, Juan Luis Martín, Fernando Olabarrieta, Enrique Arranz, and Alfredo Oliva. 2005. "A School Centered Preventative Intervention Model with Families of 2-year Old Children." XI European Conference on Developmental Psychology, Tenerife, Spain. Abstracts book.

Long, Nicholas. 2004. "E-Parenting." In *Handbook of Parenting: Theory and Research for Practice*, edited by Masud Hoghughi and Nicholas Long. London: Sage Publications.

Manzano, Ainoa, Juan Luis Martín, Fernando Olabarrieta, and Enrique Arranz. 2005a. "Servicio de prevención, formación e intervención en contextos familiares." IV Jornadas Desarrollo Humano y Educación, Alcalá De Henares, Madrid. Abstracts book.

Manzano, Ainoa, Juan Luis Martín, Fernando Olabarrieta, and Enrique Arranz. 2005b. "Family Context Prevention, Training and Intervention Service." IX. Congrès International De L'EUSARF, Enfants en Difficulté dans un Monde Difficile, Paris, France. Abstracts book.

Olabarrieta, Fernando, Enrique Arranz, Ainhoa Manzano, Juan Luis Martín, and Nuria Galende. 2009. "On Line Educational Support Service for Parents in Everyday Life with their Children." EDULEARN 09, International Conference on Education and New Learning Technologies, Barcelona. Abstracts book.

9

The Development of Values and the Media

Concepción Medrano, Ana Aierbe,
and Juan Ignacio Martínez de Morentin

From a sociocultural approach, innatism is currently no longer advocated under almost any developmental aspect, but development itself and knowledge are interpreted as something socially and culturally constructed. Framing the topic of values from this standpoint implies understanding that neither intelligence nor kindness are inherited, and that it is the capabilities of people interacting with their context explain and shape what we have become. From this approach, we believe that the act of educating is in itself evaluative. Currently, moreover, we want it to be intentional. However, to be able to respond to the demand of values education that our society advocates, certain steps are necessary that go beyond designing and scheduling curricular matters, knowing how to incorporate into the daily routine of school and community life the work entailed by the development of values.

As professionals in the field of education, we know that it is not easy to balance the achievement of well-being for all individuals (one of the goals of the current policy on well-being) and the demands of individual freedom. Thus, values that are apparently mutually opposed, such as individuality or community, are not always easy to incorporate into our vital or educational ideas. For example, in modern economically developed societies there is a marked tendency toward individualism. These issues trigger a major change in the methods of understanding and living our own lives. However, it is desirable and we believe possible to harmonize the need for individual options and the hopes and need to live in community, with the ethical commitment these proposals entail (Bauman 2001, 72).

Indeed, in the official decree that establishes basic education, we find under goals the need to address this issue, specifically the need to "make use of information technologies, as well as the media, in the process of learning and acquisition of new knowledge, with a critical sense regarding messages received and developed."[1] This involves a contribution and commitment on the part of all institutions and agents in the educational system to the proper utilization of media and information technologies.

In the development of values education, we feel it is important that, in addition to family and school, consideration be given to the different models transmitted through the media. In our opinion, the media also have a bearing on the construction of values because the models they transmit are not just personal styles; they are involved in establishing trends in society. The values transmitted are not neutral; they show specific options in life and a particular scale of values, which does not always coincide with desirable values from an educational perspective (Medrano and de la Caba 1994). In fact, many televised stories are based on behaviors arising from what we understand as countervalues. For example, very young children exhibit conduct that mimics the behaviors and attitudes they observe in any cartoon series. For example, the Japanese animation series *Shin-chan* gave rise to behaviors in children in preschool and elementary school that involved values far removed from those encouraged in families and within the classrooms. A lack of responsibility, disrespect, and an absence of the sense of duty are some of the values transmitted in the behavior of the young eponymous protagonist of the series, *Shin-chan*. Children find this very appealing and funny, and imitate it in their daily settings and with their groups of friends.

We know that historical narratives convey an image of society with its moral characteristics. Here, the "narrator's" own ethics are essential. The narrator needs to be aware of professional limitations in the process of transmiting information and try to be as honest as possible. Although postmodernity has generated considerable misgivings toward the moral authority of the narrators of televised stories, the industry's ratings grow every day, exerting a greater influence than written information.

From an educational perspective it is important to be aware of the power and moral authority exerted by the media. Failing to take advantage

---

1. Decree 175/2007 of October 16, on the Basic Education Curriculum of the Autonomous Community of the Basque Country, *Boletín Oficial del Estado* (BOE, Official State Gazette) 26035, November 13, 2007.

of the opportunities these media offer us can make us become irresponsible educators in the eyes of the new generations (Bryant and Zillmann 2002, 125; Bryant and Vorderer 2008, 257). This makes us reflect on the need to teach the youngest children to decode the messages, or in the words of Paulino Castells, to be able to "turn the sock inside out" (2002, 181). Castells suggests that we convert into educational material everything that appears not to have any didactic value. If we are capable of contextualizing within a sociohistorical and interpersonal framework, the various televised stories, benefitting from the ability to reflect so that the context in reference becomes intellectually accessible, televised content can become educational material. In this sense, it is essential to deconstruct the cultural and historical codes that generate, for example, violence or other topics that can be worked on in education. Thus, it is possible to explain to minors who generally passively visualize these images, the relevance of morally based criticism of such content.

According to certain authors (Buckingham 2003, 85; Calvert and Kotler 2003) television is a medium, as others before it, that represents the myth of current society through narrative, without having to seek an objective reality as is the case with science. One must differentiate between the conditions of manipulation and cultural alienation of a communications medium such as television, and all the aspects of cultural novelty, aesthetics and *transmission* of values that can be worked on from an educational perspective. During childhood and adolescence what is learned is what is lived through in terms of values, and in this regard, television is a vicarious source of learning. Films such as *Pulp Fiction* or *Amores perros* greatly appeal to the same adolescents who might be participating in a school intervention program aimed at improving participatory skills within the school community or the value of commitment and effort as necessary elements for their comprehensive development. In this regard, it becomes necessary to explain these types of contradictions and ambiguities, and work on them by means of different techniques in the classroom.

In other words, television also has its own educating potential, and many of its harmful effects can be minimized if it does not take up the entire leisure time of our youngest children, as well as being combined with other types of activities such as practicing sports, helping with household chores, reading, playing in the neighborhood, and being with the family. Television competes with both family and school, not only in terms of conveying information but also when it comes to *learning values*. In a way, it could be said that television offers a curriculum parallel to that of the family or school and, in some instances, might present conflicting values or even antivalues. Indeed, we see awareness of this an early and important positioning step (Medrano and Aierbe 2008).

Nevertheless, the fact that televised stories generate new meaning can only be understood if we comprehend that they do not represent "closed" content, but instead are characteristic of the media attempting to seek some response from the spectator. Through guided dialogue the closed content of television can be reconstructed to develop new meaning.

In short, audiovisual culture should provide the opportunity to create an enriching process for the viewer, distancing him or herself from just passively receiving content. This represents a challenge for the entire educational community and we should not blame mass media for the cultural impoverishment of new generations, but rather use the medium itself to further some of the values that are the basis for their development as individuals and citizens.

Within this general theoretical framework and as part of a broader study, we will now present as a summary the three core elements supporting the empirical work carried out in the Comunidad Autónoma del País Vasco/Euskal Autonomia Erkidegoa (CAPV/EAE, Autonomous Community of the Basque Country). These core elements are: television and the development of values, the socializing function of television, and value analysis using Shalom Schwartz and Klaus Boehnke's model (the Schwartz model hereafter, 2004).

Television and the Development of Values

Nowadays, bringing up the issue of whether television influences the development of values, or if the same medium reflects society's values can be paradoxical. Materialistic and prosocial values do exist in society, and they are broadcast on television. And it often transmits values contrary to those pursued by the educational curriculum. Nevertheless, we need to recognize that the power and appeal of television is very important and plays an essential role in the development and acquisition of values by our youth. Some authors (Bryant and Vorderer 2008, 125) argue that our most important narrative frame of reference is television and in some cases it forms the center of our life. However, in reviewing prior work on the impact of television on the development of values, it is evident that research is scarce and contains major gaps. This medium, in addition to serving as amusement and entertainment, also needs to educate. Yet currently it does so in both directions. We know that television transmits materialistic as well as prosocial values, and we believe this ambiguity is harmful from the standpoint of moral education (Medrano and Cortés 2007; Medrano, Aierbe, and Palacios 2008).

In this regard, several studies in the United States (for example, Tan et al. 1997) have demonstrated that television transmits conventional American middle-class values: being honest, working hard on a job well done, and a sense of duty. Along the same lines, Melanie Wakefield and colleagues (2003), in addition to stating that mass media reflect society's prevailing values, also prove that through television it is possible to encourage detrimental habits and also to give them up. In other words, television can also be used in a positive sense to encourage healthy habits and promote prosocial values. We believe this potentially positive use of television to be important and it leads us to consider the possibilities of working on values from within the media themselves.

Furthermore, other authors have analyzed certain characters that have appeared in films, and confirm their theses that media such as television and cinema are relevant in the creation of moral standards, as well as in other aspects of shaping personality (Carr 2006; Rivadeneyra and Lebo 2008). In fact, watching films is a strategy for moral education. Further, Amanda Lee (2007) in a study that analyzes the influence of television on the moral development of a group of eighteen to twenty-four year-olds, proves that television content exerts an influence on the development of values. Along the same lines, Michael Morgan (2007) raises the point that television can affect not only values, but also behaviors of youth, in terms of what they purchase, how they dress and act, how they define their identity, and how they come to understand their place in the world.

In short, on the basis of prior studies, we start from a hypothesis that television content constitutes, in itself, an avenue for learning by means of the narratives it presents. It is possible to teach and learn values through these narratives. However, we should not forget that viewers incorporate the information they receive through different contexts, so culturization does not happen unidirectionally since an interaction exists between the contexts of development and the messages.

The Socializing Function of Television

Television plays an essential role in socialization, not only in terms of information acquisition, but also in the adoption of behavioral models through the characters appearing in various programs. In this sense, Sally Steenland (1990, 35) finds that programs shown during prime time convey the idea that image is more important than intelligence, and that female characters appear to be more passive and less individualized than their male counterparts. This study also finds that adolescents identify with the values conveyed in those programs.

One study analyzes the importance of the physical attractiveness of televised models in descriptions and preferences made by children and adolescents, who were divided into three age groups (eight, fourteen and seventeen years of age), and asked to evaluate twelve previously selected models of both genders. The findings show that physical attractiveness appears as a desirable feature for all age groups (Ruiz, Conde, and Torres 2005). This study also concludes that in terms of the participants' desire to resemble these models, they all preferred the most attractive ones, which demonstrates that physical attractiveness is deemed a priority social value, even when unrelated to values such as altruism or generosity.

A study by Jake Harwood (1997) comparing different age groups (children, youth, and adults) finds a greater preference for those television or film characters of their respective age group. Young people are willing to watch television series or films featuring characters of older age groups, provided these are not involved in romantic relationships. In the same vein, this study proves that young people prefer to watch young characters on television. This study also demonstrates that programs directed at youth feature an excessive amount of characters aged twenty through fifty-nine, while the extremes in the life cycle (children and seniors) are underrepresented.

Along these lines, Cristina Persegani and colleagues (2002) find that children were systematically attributing positive behaviors and emotions to those characters they would enjoy imitating. Referring now to commercials shown on television, a study by Byoungkwann Lee, Bong-Chul Kim, and Sangpil Han (2006) that analyzed 2,295 prime time televised commercials, (859 from the United States and 1,436 from South Korea), aimed at analyzing differences between these two countries in terms of presenting senior citizens on television, finds in both countries that seniors appeared at a lower rate than their actual presence within the current population. A similar finding results from the study by Lynn Sudbury and Fiona Wilberforce (2006), where results reveal that persons of color are currently underrepresented in television commercials in the United Kingdom.

Similarly, Saito Shinichi (2007) asks whether television fosters attitudes connected with traditional gender roles, thereby helping maintain the status quo. The study shows that television tends to slow down social change, since it cultivates traditional views among a large number of viewers, especially women.

In addition, the televised series has been studied as transmitter of values from a sociological perspective. It has been shown that the social values embodied in fictionalized series' characters at times transfer to viewers. Indeed, for Yolanda Montero there are cases where a topic dealt with in a television series has achieved higher levels of social awareness than specific advertising campaigns or actual information on that topic (2006, 180).

A central aspect in most of the studies reviewed is that the socialization capability of media content is greater to the extent that the direct experience in that regard is lesser.

The Schwartz Model for the Analysis of Values

We use the model developed by Shalom Schwartz and Klaus Boehnke (2004) as a starting point in our search to discover the perceived values in the programs most enjoyed by participants in our research. These authors conceptualize values as cognitive representations originating in basic biological needs, in social interaction needs, and in the demands of various social institutions. According to Schwartz, the structure of values or domains is organized along two dimensions: one, openness to change (self-direction, stimulation, and hedonism) versus conservation (tradition, conformity, and security) and the other, self-enhancement (accomplishment and power) versus self-transcendence (universalism and benevolence). This structure of values allows us to interpret the behaviors visualized in the televised stories according to values. This model can be considered as a convergence of the Rokeach (1979) model and more culturalist perspectives that have focused on categorizing values into motivational and/or content domains with the purpose of understanding the structure underlying systems of values.

Universal aspects of human psychology and interaction systems exist that are present in all cultures, and at the same time become universal pivotal points that articulate human values systems. This model has the enormous advantage of offering a solid classification, both from a theoretical-conceptual perspective, and because it also contains a statistical-experimental validation that can greatly facilitate the analysis of values in televised stories quantitatively.

Schwartz's Values Questionnaire consists of fifty-six items that represent ten different domains or value types inferred, taking into account his theory on human motivations. From the transcultural application of this tool and turning to the technique of analyzing minimal space, findings show that the values system is likely structured upon two basic dimensions: self-enhancement versus self-transcendence, and openness to change versus conserving the status quo, in which ten types of values would be situated that were previously known as motivational domains (universalism, benevolence, tradition, conformity, security, power, accomplishment, hedonism, stimulation, and self-direction).

The structure of values presented by this model, offers an outline for interpreting behaviors visualized within televised content in terms of values. Although it is not a theory in the strict sense, we believe that it provides an outline by categories, thereby aiding the development of an empirical study.

Method

The main goal of this study was to understannd the values and certain aspects of the profile of television consumers, as well as analyzing the relationships between the values and this profile in a sample of 1,318 participants from the CAPV/EAE. We therefore set ourselves the following specific goals: (1) learn the personal values of the sample studied; (2) probe reasons for selecting favorite programs; (3) describe the characters in the subjects' favorite programs; (4) learn the motives and/or reasons for the subjects' selection of their favorite character; and (5) relate values (goal 1) with the rest of the variables analyzed (goals 2, 3, and 4).

Participants

The sample consisted of a total of 1,318 individuals, of which 73.5 percent (969) were adolescents, 12 percent (158) were young adults, and 14.5 percent (191) were adults/parents. The sampling took place after obtaining informed consent. The adolescents were secondary education students, distributed among nine schools in the CAPV/EAE (Araba, Gipuzkoa, and Bizkaia), between thirteen and fifteen years of age. The young adults were university students, between nineteen and thirty years of age. Finally, the parents group, obtained through the adolescents, ranged in ages from thirty to fify-five.

Measuring Instruments

This study used two instruments submitted within the same report booklet. The first part included items concenring the participants' profile as consumers and the reasons they provided to justify their selection of certain programs, as well as their favorite characters, through the Television Viewing Habits Questionnaire, created and validated by our research group with high internal consistency (Cronbach's alpha = 0.93). The questionnaire consisted of thirty items, twenty-four of them closed, and the remaining six open. The six open items covered aspects related to: the programs they most enjoy and their argument as to why, programs they enjoy watching at home but are not allowed to, programs they most often watch, and how they identify with the characters in the programs they most and least enjoy. For this presentation, responses to item 20 ("What are your reasons for liking those programs?"); to item 24 ("Which character is your favorite?"), and to item 24 b ("Reasons and arguments for selecting that character."), were put into categories.

In the second part of the report booklet subjects were shown the Television Viewing Value Domain Scale (Val-TV 0.1), used to understand the perceived values in their favorite television programs. This instrument is an adaptation of the Value Scale originally created by Schwartz (SVS). The scores referring to the values were obtained by responding to the ten items in each subscale pertaining to the values of: self-direction, stimulation, hedonism, achievement, power, security, conformity, tradition, benevolence, and universalism. These scores were collected by means of a five point Lickert scale, which indicates the level of agreement or disagreement with each item. This scale was statistically validated through multidimensional analysis, and structurally it is an almost exact replica of the original model. However, the index obtained is not very high (Cronbach's alpha = 0.615), which indicates that the correlation between value domains is moderate; in other words, we have items measuring different things.

Procedure

The process of administering both instruments took about sixty minutes. Data gathering, in the case of adolescents, was carried out by the researchers themselves together with a teacher from the school, and in other cases by the instructors responsible for each classroom. Under live testing conditions each adolescent was given two questionnaires, one for the father and another for the mother, in a sealed envelope together with an explanatory letter of the study goals. Sampling data from the youth, all university students in the Basque Country, were obtained online. Both quantitative and statistical analyses were then made. In addition, and this was the most demanding part of the task, for purposes of qualitative analyses of the open questions three phases were followed to facilitate the categorizing of all responses obtained.

During the first phase a transcript was made of all the responses. During the second phase categories of analysis arising from the text were created. Categories were then refined, taking into consideration two criteria: experimentation and the theoretical criterion. After the fact and qualitatively, all categories were defined. In a first selection for item 20 ("Why do you like those programs?") thirteen categories were established and defined. These categories were: action, entertainment, fun-humor, information-current events, educational, actors/hosts/characters, contents, schedule, topic of conversation, family consensus, nothing selected, real-life (identification), and other. Likewise, for item 24a ("Which is your favorite character in the programs you watch the most?") and item 24 b ("Why?"), eighteen categories or cores of analyses were defined and categorized after the fact, which allowed us to determine what television genre the selected character came from, to wit: series (police, historical, comedy, or by occupation via trades and professions), sports, cartoons, soap operas, news reports, films, celebrity gossip, talk shows, late night shows, reality shows, game shows, cultural, humor, and others. Furthermore, responses were also grouped taking into consideration the following aspects: gender of the selected character; the developmental stage of the character, that is, where appropriate: childhood, adolescence, adulthood, and/or senior citizens; the development of the character's role in a program based on fiction or reality; and finally, whether or not the character performs a trade or job. In other words, besides the television genre he or she belongs to, we had four other features of the selected character that provided us with relevant qualitative information on that choice's features. In order to systematize and categorize the answers regarding item 24b (the "Whys?"), given the huge variety of responses, twenty-one cores of analysis or subcategories were defined and established, to wit: entertainment, boredom, positive physical attributes, negative physical attributes, social skills, clumsiness, being conventional, being nonconventional, professionalism, lack of professionalism, intelligence, lack of intelligence, positive personality, negative personality, unspecified personality, prestige, lack of prestige, personally identifying with the character, not personally identifying with the character, cultural identity, and no cultural identity. All categories were defined and compared by means of a collective reading by three judges. Cohen's Kappa coefficient of agreement was 0.7.

During a third phase and in order to make statistically manageable the high number of key themes extracted, these themes were recategorized. The criterion selected in this case was to regroup those categories that rated a lower percentage of responses, and to group them by following a theoretical criterion related to the content of the category. Thus, in the case of item 20, grouped under the category of "other" were the responses from the categories of action (0.4 percent of the response), consensus (0.1 percent), nothing selected (0.3 percent), real-life (1.7 percent), educational (2.1 percent), actors/hosts/characters (1.0 percent), schedule (0.3 percent), and topic of conversation (0.2 percent).

In the specific case of characters from television series (item 24a), several categories were grouped into two new categories. Specifically appearing as "general series and films" are the subcategories of unspecified series (1.7 percent), films (1.4 percent), and historical series (0.3 percent), and as "news programs and shows" are those of celebrity gossip (0.3 percent), talk shows (0.1 percent), late night shows (2.1 percent), and reality shows (0.4 percent). As far as reasons why they like those characters (item 24b), the changes involved regrouping those of lesser frequency under three new categories: "other negative features" (lack of intelligence [4.1 percent], negative personality [0.8 percent], unspecified personality [3.3 percent], clumsiness or lack of social skills [0.7 percent]); "other positive features" (intelligence [2.9 percent], prestige [2.3 percent], social skills [0.3 percent], being conventional [0.3 percent]); and "personally identifying with the character" (personally identifying [2.6 percent], cultural identity [0.2 percent], and no cultural identity [0.2 percent]).

Results

We will now discuss the results obtained from this study of the profiles of television consumers, with particular reference to their values and certain other dimensions. Our discussion is based on the previously noted goals we outlined prior to undertaking the study.

Goal 1

Regarding our first goal, learning what their personal values are, as can be seen in table 9.1, the highest scores were in benevolence, conformity, and self-direction; these surpassed four points in a scale with a maximum of five. On the other hand, the lowest scores appeared in the power value, which did not reach the theoretical mean score of three points on the scale. The rest reflected scores between three and four.

Table 9.1. Descriptive statistics: value scale

Descriptor	N	Mean	Standard deviation
Self-direction	1197	4.01	1.053
Stimulation	1194	3.59	1.086
Hedonism	1191	3.93	1.080
Achievement	1193	3.88	1.084
Power	1190	2.76	1.214
Security	1192	3.90	1.065
Conformity	1191	4.04	1.046
Tradition	1192	3.60	1.630
Benevolence	1189	4.14	1.043
Universalism	1191	3.92	1.057

Goals 2, 3, and 4

Regarding the second, third and fourth goals, the sample positioned itself differently in terms of television. The most frequent reason for selecting programs (item 20, "Why do you like these programs?") was due to positive content (40.3 percent), followed at a considerably distant percentage by programs dealing with fun-humor (22.2 percent) or entertainment (18.9 percent). Further down was the category of contents (8 percent), news-current events (4.5 percent), and the rest of the programs not included under other categories (6.1 percent). Favorites above all are characters in comedy series (29.2 percent) and in cartoons (23.8 percent), followed at some distance by humorous characters (11.3 percent) and those in soap operas (10.9 percent). Being funny was the main reason for selecting a television character (43. percent), followed at a much greater distance by other reasons such as professionalism (14.4 percent), other physical qualities socially deemed as positive (11.8 percent), a positive personality (9.8 percent) or other negative features (9.2 percent). Other categories such as having positive characteristics, being easy to personally relate to, or being nonconventional, were less often selected.

Goal 5

With regards to the fifth and last goal, learning how the values of the study participants relate to their television preferences, the results appear in table 9.2. It shows the contrasting statistics for the variance analyses carried out between the different categories of television-related choices. Since age could be a conditioning factor in terms of the type of selections in television programs, age group was included as a covariate.

In principle, there were no differences in the values shown by the participants as regards the types of television programs they selected (item 20). Nevertheless, we did find some differences in the values of achievement ($F = 1,828$, $p = 0.046$) and benevolence ($F = 1,995$, $p = 0.026$) in terms of the type of character selected by participants. However, the explained variance percentages are low. Comparisons by pairs (Sidak) indicate in the first case ($p = 0.049$) only greater levels of achievement amont those selecting characters in game shows, versus those who select characters from police series (4.40 [0.764] versus 3.47 [1.298]). In the second case ($p = 0.023$), those selecting soap opera characters showed greater levels of benevolence than those who selected cartoons.

We also found some statistically significant differences in the values of self-direction ($F = 2.351$, $p = 0.022$) and tradition ($F = 2.4470$, $p = 0.016$) when inquiring as to the reasons for selecting these characters. As in the previous case, the explained variance percentages are low. Comparisons by pairs (Sidak) in this case indicate that those selecting characters because of personally identifying with them scored less in tradition than those whose based their choice on professionalism (2.85 [0.229] versus 3.772 [0.105], p=.008) or positive personality (2.85 [0.229] versus 3.658 [0.124], p=.048). In the case of self-direction, in spite of a significant contrast, there wasn't any statistically significant difference between pairs.

The selection of male or female characters is associated with differences in the value of power ($F = 4.696$, $p = 0.031$), although again with a very low explained variance percentage (0.6 percent). Those who selected male characters scored higher in power than those selecting female characters (2.82 [1.244] versus 2.58 [1.192]). The selection of characters on the basis of whether they were fictional or real was associated with differences in the value of achievement ($F = 4.008$, $p = 0.046$), with the result that those who selected real characters scored higher than those selecting fictional ones (4.11 [0.995] versus 3.92 [1.086]). There were no score differences in values for the rest of variables considered, age group of the television character selected or whether the character was involved in a professional activity or not.

Table 9.2. Variance analysis on the sample's selections regarding television programs

	Type of programs (Item 20)	Character from the programs (Item 24a)	Reasons for selecting a program (Item 24b)	Character gender female	Character age	Character nature	Character occupation
	F	F	F	F	F	F	F
Self-direction	.934	1.440	2.351*	0.096	1.213	0.015	0.111
Stimulation	0.131	1.509	0.725	1.052	2.051	2.251	0.933
Hedonism	1.676	1.249	0.871	3.320	0.310	2.961	0.002
Achievement	1.012	1.828*	1.994	2.983	1.387	4.008*	0.001
Power	1.555	1.533	.786	4.696*	1.007	2.596	0.453
Security	1.033	1.125	1.418	0.832	0.243	0.584	0.221
Conformity	1.967	1.659	0.988	0.124	1.857	0.022	0.383
Tradition	1.950	0.939	2.470*	0.079	0.272	1.408	1.480
Benevolence	0.275	1.995*	1.912	0.424	0.657	0.316	1.029
Universalism	1.002	1.301	1.464	2.261	1.391	0.153	0.463

* $P < 0.05$

Conclusion

Taking all the data as a whole, the first conclusion we draw is the large diversity of preferences with respect to values in watching television. Within this variety of preferences, we found certain differences in the values of the people we studied in the CAPV/EAE. Thus, we found that their values are not included within a single domain (along the lines of Schwartz) but rather, the trend is heterogeneous. This might be explained by what we previously noted in our introduction regarding the ambiguity that exists in current society, where prosocial as well as materialistic values coexist. In this sense, Basque society within a Western context is not exempt from this trend.

When referring to the selections made by our sample in terms of program types, characters chosen, and reasons for selecting them, there was a preference for leisure and entertainment options. One should note, moreover, that the most popular profile selected was that of the funny or humorous character. This confirms that the purpose of television is fun and entertainment, and almost never educational.

This does not mean that educational institutions cannot and should not, on the basis of the preferences shown by our Basque youth, decode the messages and work with their favorite programs. Our idea is that just as students do not attend school for entertainment purposes, so people do not watch television for purposes of learning or acquiring information. However, television stories are not unambiguous, and it is possible and advantageous to work with them as a starting point, in order to reconstruct their meaning and have a bearing on those values that we wish to impart. In short, our academic institutions have the opportunity of using television content as a source for learning, transforming not only television but the media in general into an educational tool to develop television literacy skills as well as encourange the development of values (Camps 1994, 85; López 2009, 25).

The research outlined here allows us to discuss certain educational implications. For example, achievement as a value is more relevant for those who select game shows than among those choosing police series, just as it does for those who prefer real characters as apposed to those choose fictional ones. Furthermore, power as a value scores higher when male characters are selected, whereas tradition as a value scores higher when a preferred charcetr is chosen on the grounds of professionalism. Meanwhile, benevolence is associated with soap opera characters. These data, interpreted from the Schwartz model, provide us with multiple clues for the purposes of continuing to study in greater depth issues regarding the development of values and their relationship with the media.

All in all, the relationships between personal values and our television preferences are not only confirmed by these results, but can also become a good educational resource. We believe that in the family context it is necessary to address in greater depth parental guidelines for television viewing (Aierbe, Medrano, and Orejudo 2008). And within the formal context of school, it is increasingly necessary to work on and develop the issue of responsibility with regards to television, in terms of values development (Medrano 2008b).

Nevertheless, for television consumption to be truly educational, one must know how to "read" the medium, in the same way we read written texts. In this regard, we should promote awareness of the models being transmitted and contrast them against those models we wish to educate our young people in, with a specific plan to develop values. Then, using actual television content as a starting point, for example, educational institutions can work on the various social stereotypes that this medium conveys, and proceed to decodify its messages. It is possible to promote a critical analysis of television and the development of values by means of different activities. Among these activities, it is important to point out: dialogue situations (Flecha 1997); comparison strategies (Orozco and Vassallo 2009, 267); and the reinterpretation of messages, confrontation, and formal exploration, as well as handling and interpreting the various messages (Steen and Owens 2001). Along the same lines, simulation games through certain episodes from favorite series, or characters identified with, allow teachers and students to stage the attitudes and values conveyed by that series or character, and to decode those values and attitudes by means of discussion groups (Medrano 2008a).

Therefore, one of the most relevant findings in this work, in educational terms, is the suitability of working on the basis of viewers' television preferences. We must encourage explicitness and awareness of all those values underlying the most selected television programs and characters by the various age groups, as indicated by the data collected in the Basque Country. It is not a question of creating new educational programs, but rather working on the basis of viewers' favorite programs and proceeding to systematize strategies for the development of values (Medrano 2005; Medrano and Cortés 2007).

Finally, we contend that viewing television or other media can be an opportunity to learn how to preselect, choose, and utilize our free time in accordance with our favorite programs. For us television is a medium that, if well utilized, can become an educational resource for values development. As professionals in the field of education we should consider making the most of the opportunity that educating through the different media entails, because in our society there is no other technology that reaches more homes and is more consumed by almost the entire population.

References

Aierbe, Ana, Concepción Medrano, and Santos Orejudo. 2008. "Hábitos televisivos, valores y mediación parental en adolescentes." *Revista Mexicana de Psicología* 25, no.2: 259–70.

Bauman, Zygmunt. 2001. *Community: Seeking Safety in an Insecure World*. Cambridge: Polity Press.

Bryant, Jennings, and Peter Vorderer. 2008. *Psychology of Entertainment*. New York: Routledge.

Bryant, Jennings, and Dolf Zillmann. 2002. *Media Effects: Advances in Theory and Research*. New Jersey: Lawrence Elbaum Associates.

Buckingham, David. 2003. *Media Education: Literacy, Learning and Contemporary Culture*. Cambridge: Polity Press.

Calvert, Sandra, and Jennifer Kotler. 2003. "Lessons from Children's Television: The Impact of the Children's Television Act on Children's Learning." *Applied Developmental Psychology* 24, no.1: 275–35.

Camps, Victoria. 1994. *Los valores de la educación*. Madrid: Alauda-Anaya.

Carr, David. 2006. "Moral Education at the Movies: On the Cinematic Treatment of Morally Significant Story and Narrative." *Journal of Moral Education* 35, no.3: 319–33.

Castells, Paulino. 2002. *Enganchados a las pantallas. Televisión, videojuegos, Internet y móviles*. Barcelona: Planeta.

Decreto 175/2007 de Octubre del Currículo de la Educación Básica de la Comunidad Autónoma del País Vasco. *Boletín Oficial del Estado*. N. 26035 of November 13, 2007.

Flecha, Ramón. 1997. *Compartiendo palabras. El aprendizaje de las personas adultas a través del diálogo*. Barcelona: Paidós.

Harwood, Jake. 1997. "Viewing Age: Lifespan Identity and Television Viewing Choices." *Journal of Broadcasting and Electronic Media* 41, no. 2: 203–13.

Lee, Amanda. 2007. "The Role of Television on Moral Development from the Perspective of the Young Adult." *Dissertation, Abstracts, International. Section A: Humanities and Social Sciences* 68, no.6: 22–26.

Lee, Byoungkwann, Bong-Chul Kim, and Sangpil Han. "The Portrayal of Older People in Television Advertisements: A Cross-Cultural Content Analysis of the United States and South Korea." *International Journal of Aging and Human Development* 63, no.1 (2006): 279–97.

López, Félix. 2009. *Las emociones en educación.* Madrid: Morata.

Medrano, Concepción. 2005. "¿Se puede favorecer el aprendizaje de valores a través de la televisión?" *Revista de Educación* 338, no.1: 245–70.

———. 2008a. "¿Qué valores perciben los adolescentes en sus programas favoritos de T.V?" *Comunicar. Latin American Scientific Journal of Media Education* 31, no.1: 387–92.

———. 2008b. "Televisión y educación: del entretenimiento al aprendizaje." *Teoría de la educación* 20, no.1: 205–24.

Medrano, Concepción, and María Angeles De La Caba. 1994. "A Model of Intervention for Improving Moral Reasoning: An Experiment in the Basque Country." *Journal of Moral Education* 23, no.1: 427–37.

Medrano, Concepción, and Alejandra Cortés. 2007. "The Teaching and Learning of Values through Television." *International Review of Education* 53, no.1: 5–21.

Medrano, Concepción, Ana Aierbe, and Santiago Palacios. 2008. "La dieta televisiva y los valores. Un estudio realizado con adolescentes en la Comunidad Autónoma del País Vasco." *Revista Española de Pedagogía* 239, no.1: 65–84.

Medrano, Concepción, and Ana Aierbe. 2008. "Valores y contextos de desarrollo." *Psicodidáctica* 13, no.1: 53–68.

Montero, Yolanda. 2006. *Televisión, valores y adolescencia.* Barcelona: Gedisa.

Morgan, Michael. 2007. "What do Young People Learn about the World from Watching Television?" In *20 Questions about youth and the media*, edited by Sharon R. Mazzarella. New York: Peter Lang Publishing.

Orozco, Guillermo and María Inmaculada Vassallo. 2009. *La ficción televisiva en Iberoamérica. Narrativas, formatos y publicidad.* Guadalajara (México): Ediciones de la Noche.

Persegani, Cristina, Pierluigi Russo, Cristina Carucci, Marisa Nicolini, Luciana Luisa Papeschi, and Michele Trimarchi. 2002. "Television Viewing and Personality Structure in Children." *Personality and Individual Differences* 32, no.1: 977–90.

Rivadeneyra, Rocío, and Melanie Lebo. 2008. "The Association Between Television-Viewing Behaviors and Adolescent Dating Role Attitudes and Behaviors." *Journal of Adolescence* 31, no.1: 291-305.

Rokeach, Milton. 1979. *Understanding Human Values: Individual and Societal.* New York: Free Press.

Ruiz, Cristina, Elena Conde, and Esteban Torres. 2005. "Importance of Facial Physical Attractiveness of Audiovisual Models in Descriptions and Preferences of Children and Adolescents." *Perceptual and Motor Skills* 101, no.1: 229–43.

Schwartz, Shalom, and Klaus Boehnke. 2004. "Evaluating the Structure of Human Values with Confirmatory Factor Analysis." *Journal of Research in Personality* 38, no.1: 230–55.

Shinichi, Saito. 2007. "Television and the Cultivation of Gender-Role Attitudes in Japan: Does Television Contribute to the Maintenance of the Status Quo?" *Journal of Communication* 57, no.3: 511–31.

Steen, Francis, and Stephanie Owens. 2001. "Evolution's Pedagogy: An Adaptionist Model of Pretense and Entertainment." *Journal of Cognition and Culture* 1, no.1: 289–321.

Steenland, Sally. 1990. *La educación en la programación en las horas de mayor audiencia. Un análisis sobre las adolescentes en la televisión.* Madrid: Comunidad de Madrid, Dirección General de la Mujer.

Sudbury, Lynn, and Fiona Wilberforce. 2006. "The Portrayal of Black People in UK Television Advertising: Perception and Reality." *Journal of Consumer Behaviour* 5, no.5: 465–76.

Tan, Alexis, Leigh Nelson, Qingwen Dong, and Gerdean Tan. 1997. "Value Acceptance in Adolescent Socialization: A Test of a Cognitive-Functional Theory of Television Effects." *Communication Monographs* 64, no.1: 82–97.

Wakfield, Melanie, Brian Flay, Mark Nichter, and Gary Giovino. 2003. "Role of the Media in Influencing Trajectories of Youth Smoking." *Addiction* 98, no.1: 79–103.

Index

mutual help, 61

N

Nahiko program, 80, 84–85

narratives, 38, 43, 148, 176, 177, 178

National Curriculum Integration Project, 111

nation-state: breakdown of, 143–44; and development of public education, 15–18, 142–43

neuropsychological maturity, 67

New Haven, Connecticut, School Development Program in, 123

no-fault problem solving, 123

O

objectors, school, 96

P

parenting schools, 161

Parentline Plus, 163

parents: challenges of, 159–60; counseling and education service for, 159–73; disciplinary breaches of, 94; of foreign immigrant students, 153; importance of involvement of, 145n3; information technology and, 162; seeking help from, 103; television and, 189. *See also* family counseling and education service

participation: in cooperative games, 59; in dialogue approach, 122, 129–30, 131, 135–37; in education, 155; in Learning Communities process, 127–30, 131, 134–37, 147–48; in social intervention, 70

peace: conflict resolution education to promote a culture of, 105–6; family support and, 160; psycho-educational programs to promote, 55–70

penitentiary, Learning Communities project in, 126

physical attractiveness, of television characters, 180

Pisa Reports (Programme for International Student Assessment), 29n11

Plan de Educación Especial para El País Vasco, 35

Plan for Coeducation and Prevention of Gender Violence, 86–87

plastic-constructive creativity games, 62

play, child-, research on, 56–57

police series, 187, 189

Portugalete, 167, 172

power value, 186, 187, 188, 189

primary education: gender violence in, 74, 78; gender violence prevention in, 77–87; special education in, 27–28; student body distribution in, 24; territorial supply distribution in, 25

principal, being sent to the, 101

private education: public education *versus,* 17–18, 20–21, 30–31; subsidized, 19–20. *See also* subsidized-private schools

problem-solving involvement, student perceptions of, 102

professional training programs: empirical study of, 41–42, 44–49; gender differences in, 41;

List of Contributors

For full biographical information about the contributors, links to their projects, and more, visit www.basque.unr.edu/currentresearch/contributors

Begoña Abad Miguélez
Ana Aierbe
Jone Aliri
Maria José Alonso Olea
Ramón Alzate Sáez de Heredia
Maite Arandia Loroño
Enrique Arranz Freijo
Mikel Arriaga Landeta
Nekane Beloki Arizti
Andrés Davila
Maite Garaigordobil
Aitor Gómez González
Lucía Gorbeña
Juan Luis Martín Ayala
Juan Ignacio Martínez de Morentin
Begoña Martínez Domínguez
Isabel Martínez Domínguez
Concepción Medrano
Cristina Merino
Fernando Olabarrieta Artetxe
Iñaki Santa Cruz Ayo
Alfonso Unceta

DATE DUE
